Favorite Recorder Tunes

Beautiful American Airs and Ballads

Marcia Diehl

The Rottenburgh Baroque recorder model 4204 of boxwood on our cover is courtesy of Moeck Musikinstrumente + Verlag GmbH, Celle – Germany.

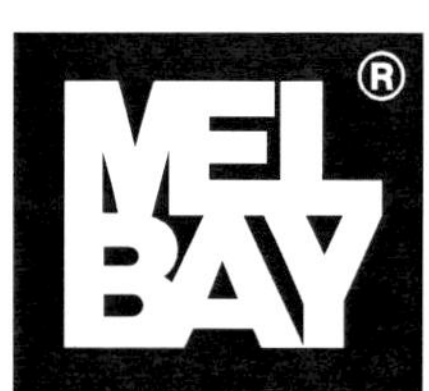

WWW.MELBAY.COM

PREFACE

Favorite Recorder Tunes/Beautiful American Airs and Ballads is a collection of 41 timeless melodies arranged for soprano and tenor recorders with suggested accompaniment chords. The book encompasses a variety of influences which collectively portray a historical and aesthetic view of the American musical landscape.

Highlighting just a few of the gems in this collection:

Civil War composers, George F. Root, J. P. Webster, and John H. Hewitt are represented by well-known themes like “Just Before the Battle, Mother”. The prolific Carrie Jacobs-Bond and Stephen Foster wrote about romantic love in “Just Awearyin’ for You” and “Slumber, My Darling”, while lesser-known songwriters, Norman Hedges and Gene Close expressed the melancholic cowboy’s loneliness on the vast panoramic plains in the song, “Sunset in the Hills”.

The American immigrant heritage is evidenced in “Jefferson and Liberty”, a slow jig with echoes of the Emerald Isle. Joseph Brackett Jr.’s Shaker tune, “Simple Gifts”, is quintessentially American and was used by Aaron Copland in his iconic orchestral composition, *Appalachian Spring*.

By contrast, Edward MacDowell formally studied music in Europe, where he lived for a lengthy time and married American Marian Griswold Nevins. Upon the couple’s return to America, he furthered his musical legacy as a composer, concert artist and music teacher. Prior to his death in 1908, Marian set up an artist residency program on their farm property in New Hampshire known as “MacDowell”. The program has supported the early careers of many musicians, artists, writers, and filmmakers. Edward MacDowell’s lovely “To a Wild Rose” is included in this collection and is familiar to many.

Finally, a riverman’s tune, “Shenandoah” —is truly one of the most beautiful songs in the American folk song repertoire. In closing, among these masterful known and unknown composers of melodies, I humbly offer my own composition, “Farewell/Adieu”.

I present this collection to you for your playing and listening pleasure, and as an opportunity to call audience attention to the rich history of *Beautiful American Airs and Ballads*.

I hope you enjoy it.

Marcia Diehl

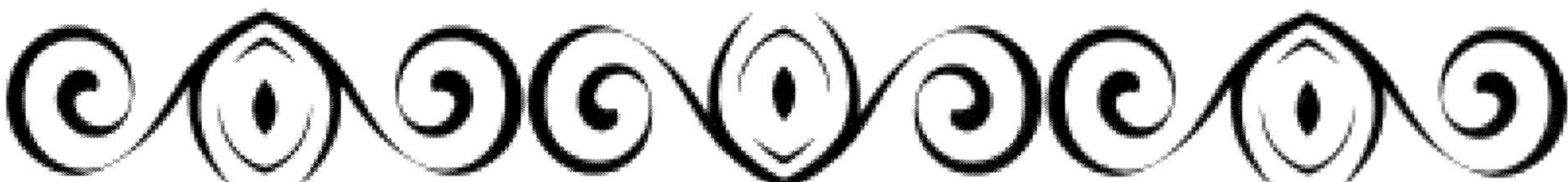

INDEX

Slumber, My Darling

Stephen Foster

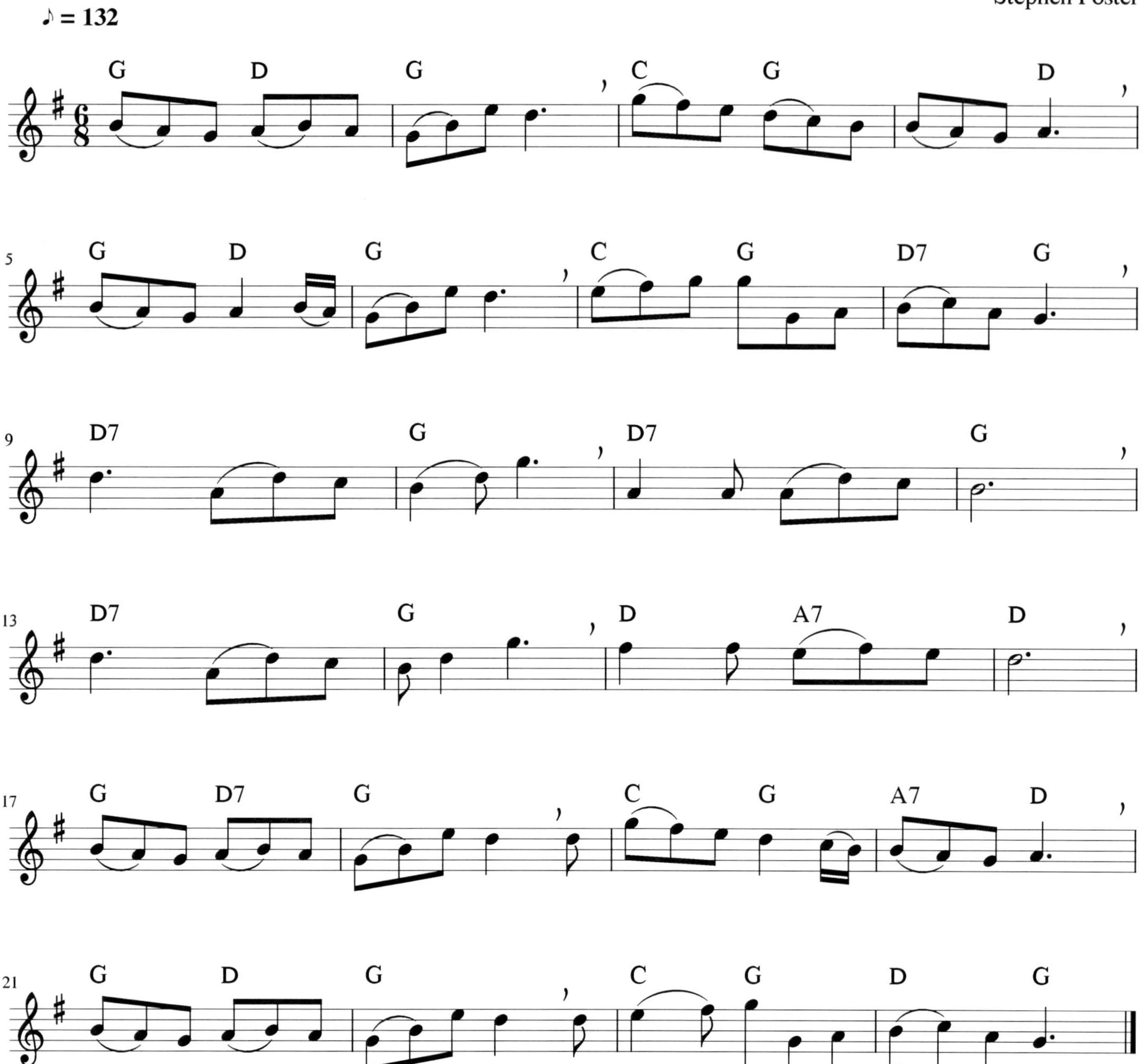

Sadly to Mine Heart Appealing

Stephen Foster

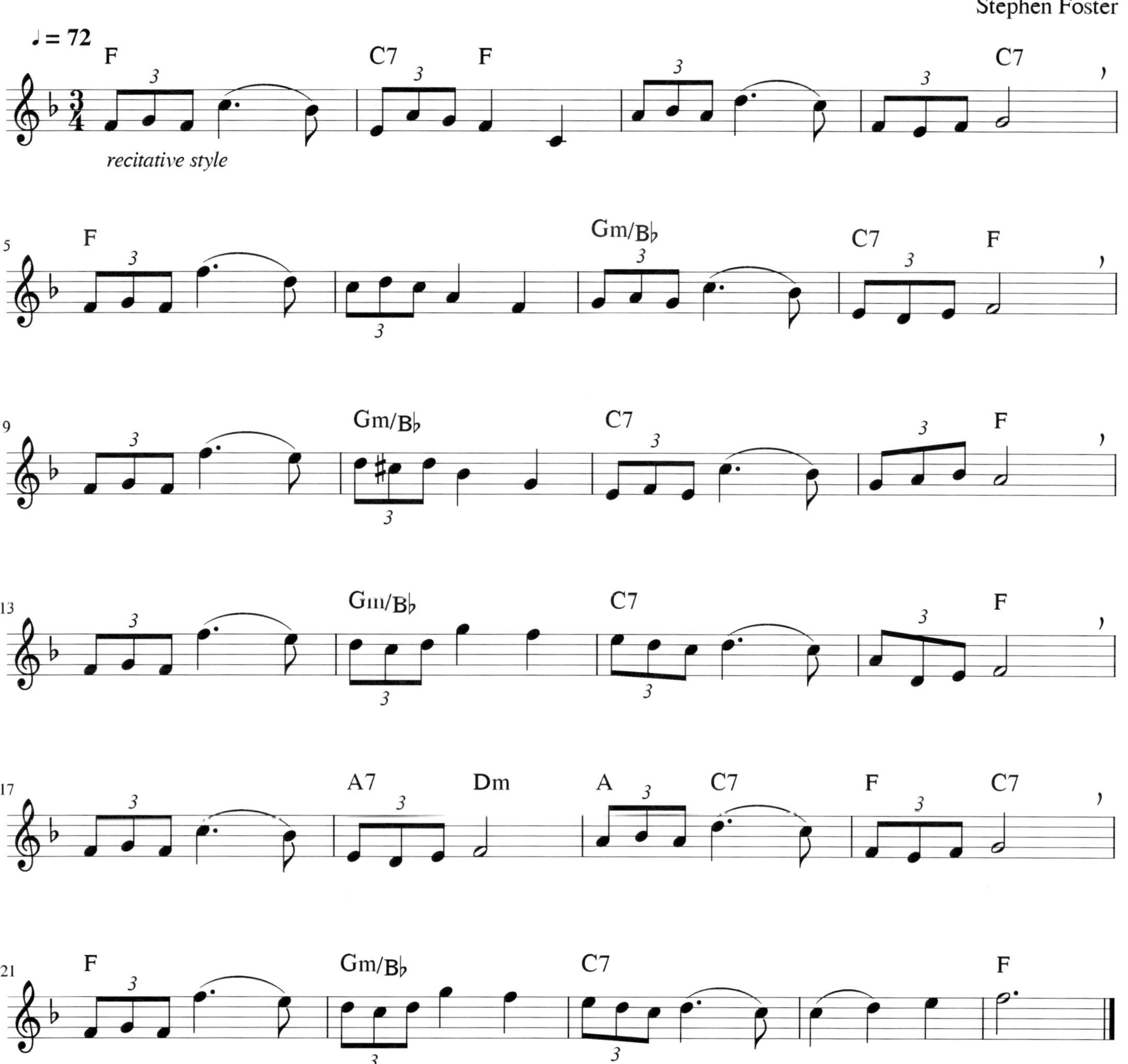

My Old Kentucky Home

Stephen Foster

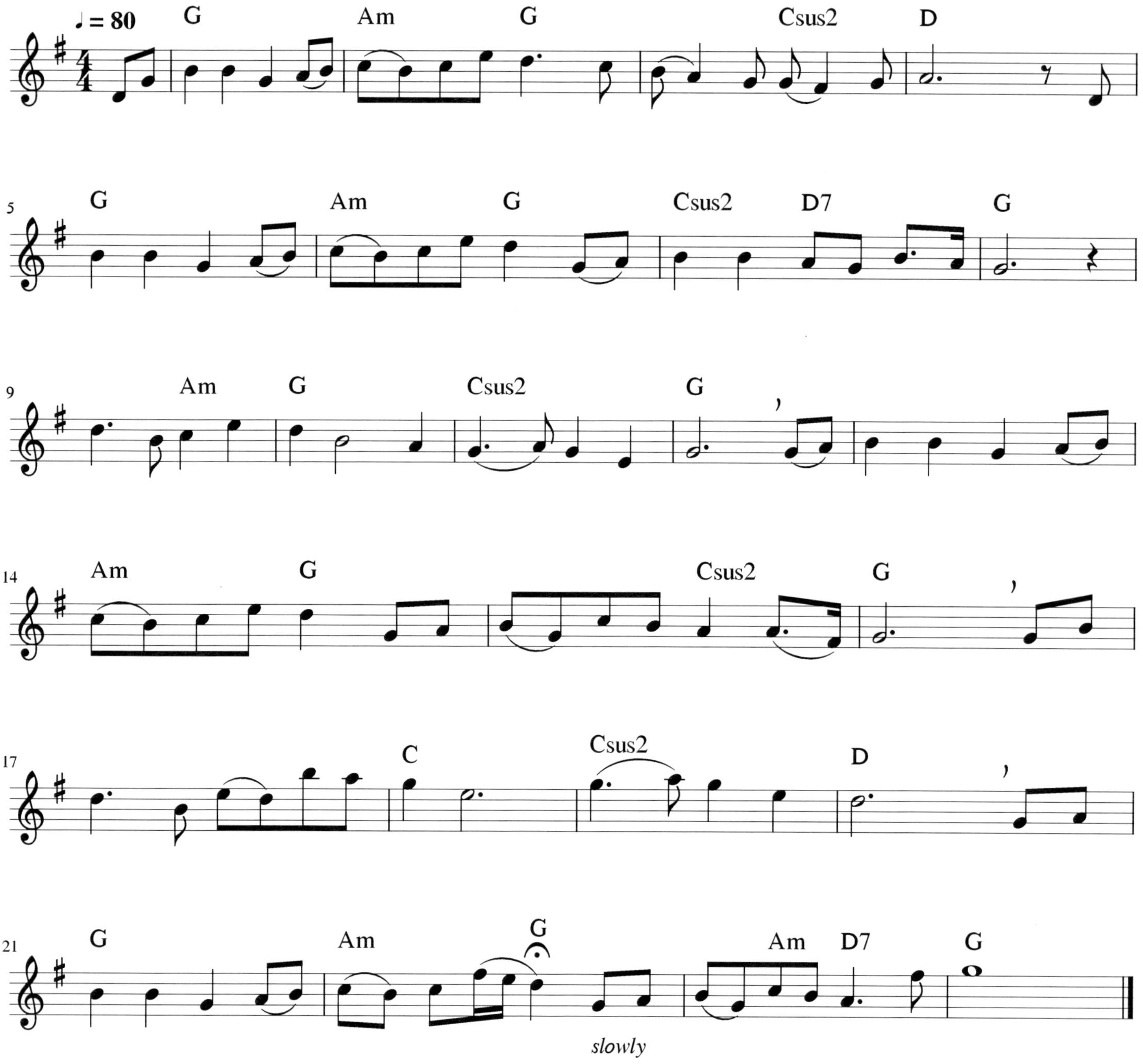

♩ = 80 G Am G Csus2 D

5 G Am G Csus2 D7 G

9 Am G Csus2 G

14 Am G Csus2 G

17 C Csus2 D

21 G Am G Am D7 G

slowly

None Shall Weep a Tear for Me

Stephen Foster

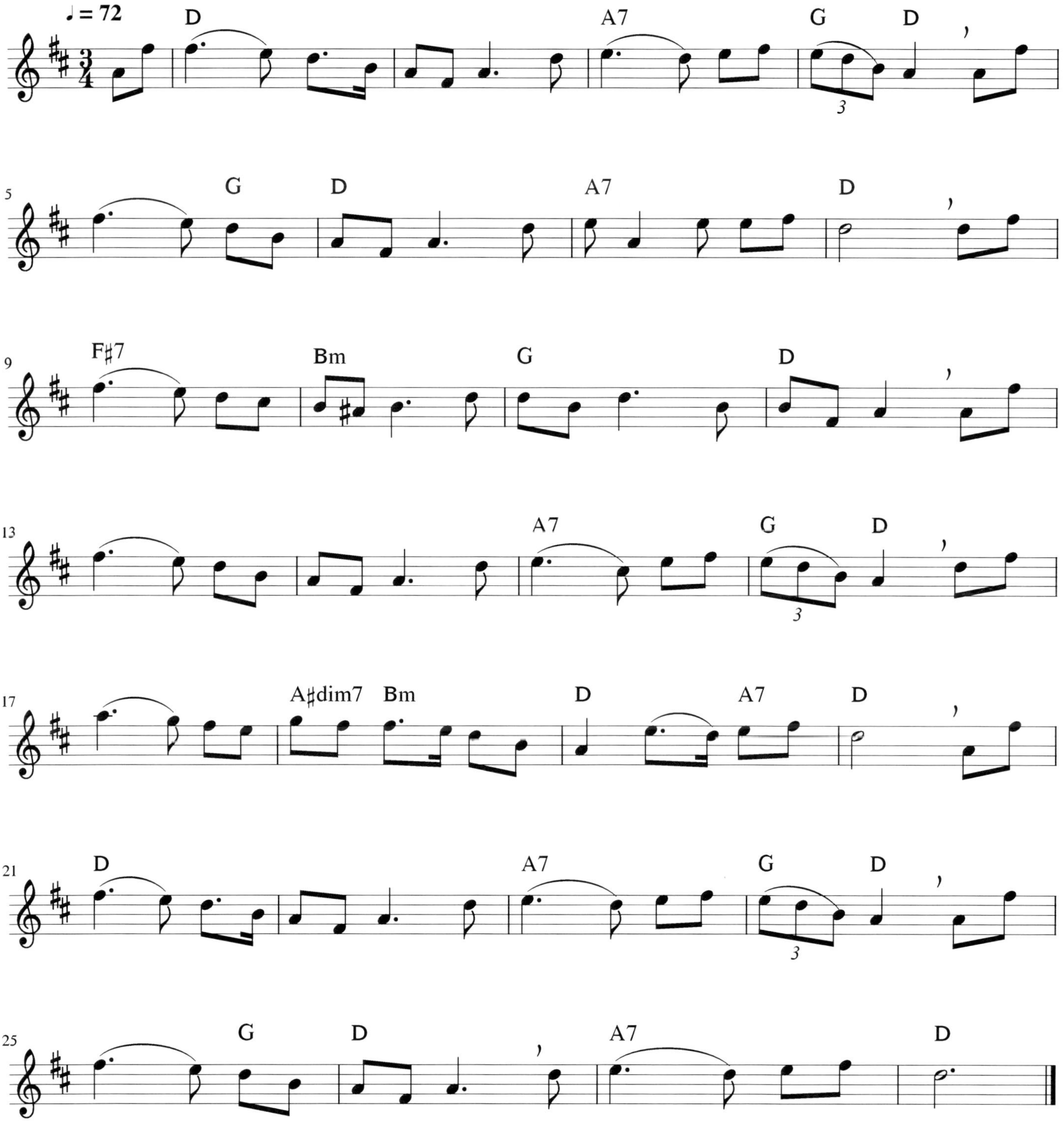

♩ = 72

D A7 G D

5 G D A7 D

9 F♯7 Bm G D

13 A7 G D

17 A♯dim7 Bm D A7 D

21 D A7 G D

25 G D A7 D

Hard Times Come Again No More

Stephen Foster

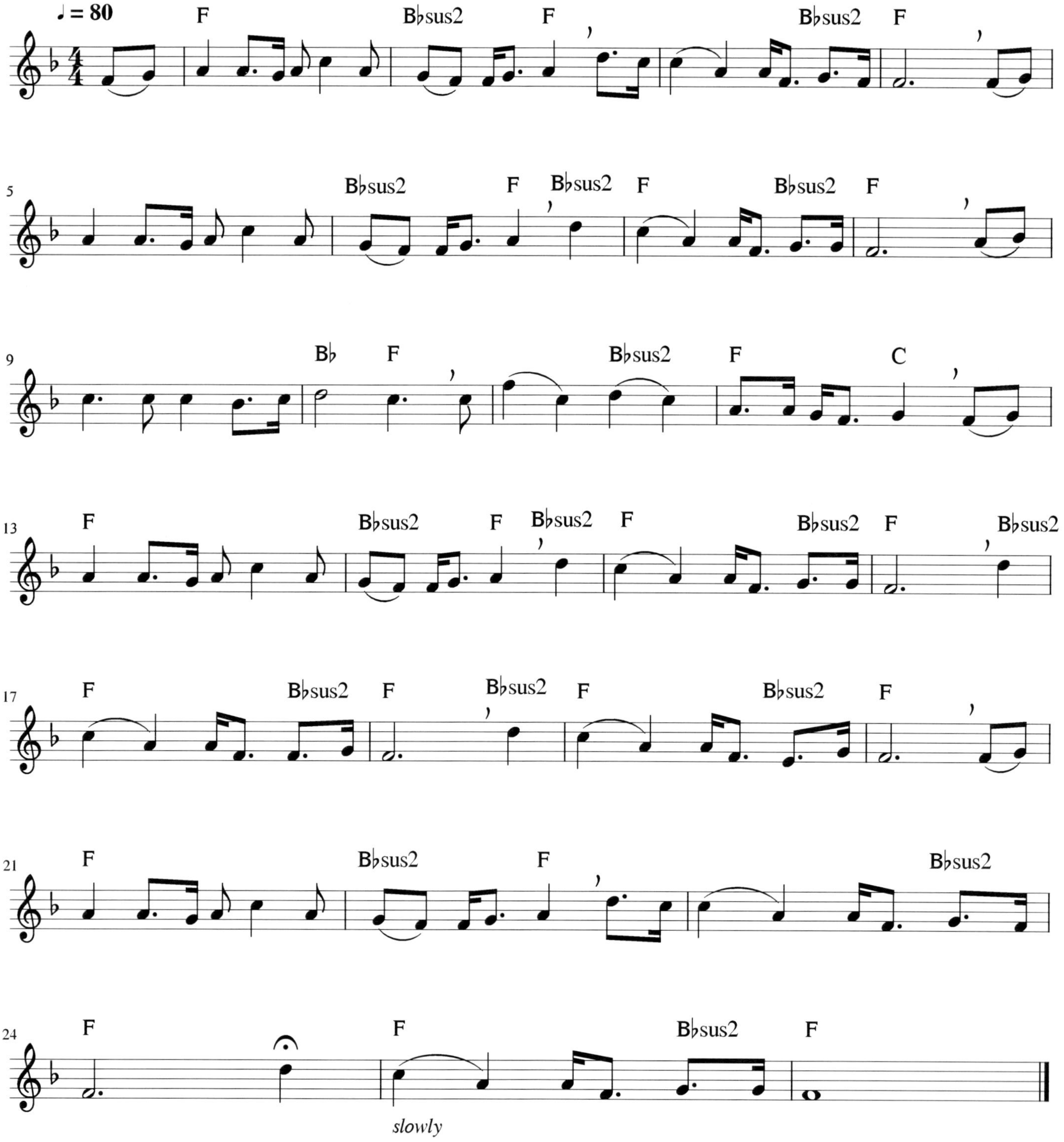

♩ = 80

F Bbsus2 F Bbsus2 F

5 Bbsus2 F Bbsus2 F Bbsus2 F

9 Bb F Bbsus2 F C

13 F Bbsus2 F Bbsus2 F Bbsus2 F Bbsus2

17 F Bbsus2 F Bbsus2 F Bbsus2 F

21 F Bbsus2 F Bbsus2

24 F F Bbsus2 F

slowly

I Will Be True to Thee

Stephen Foster

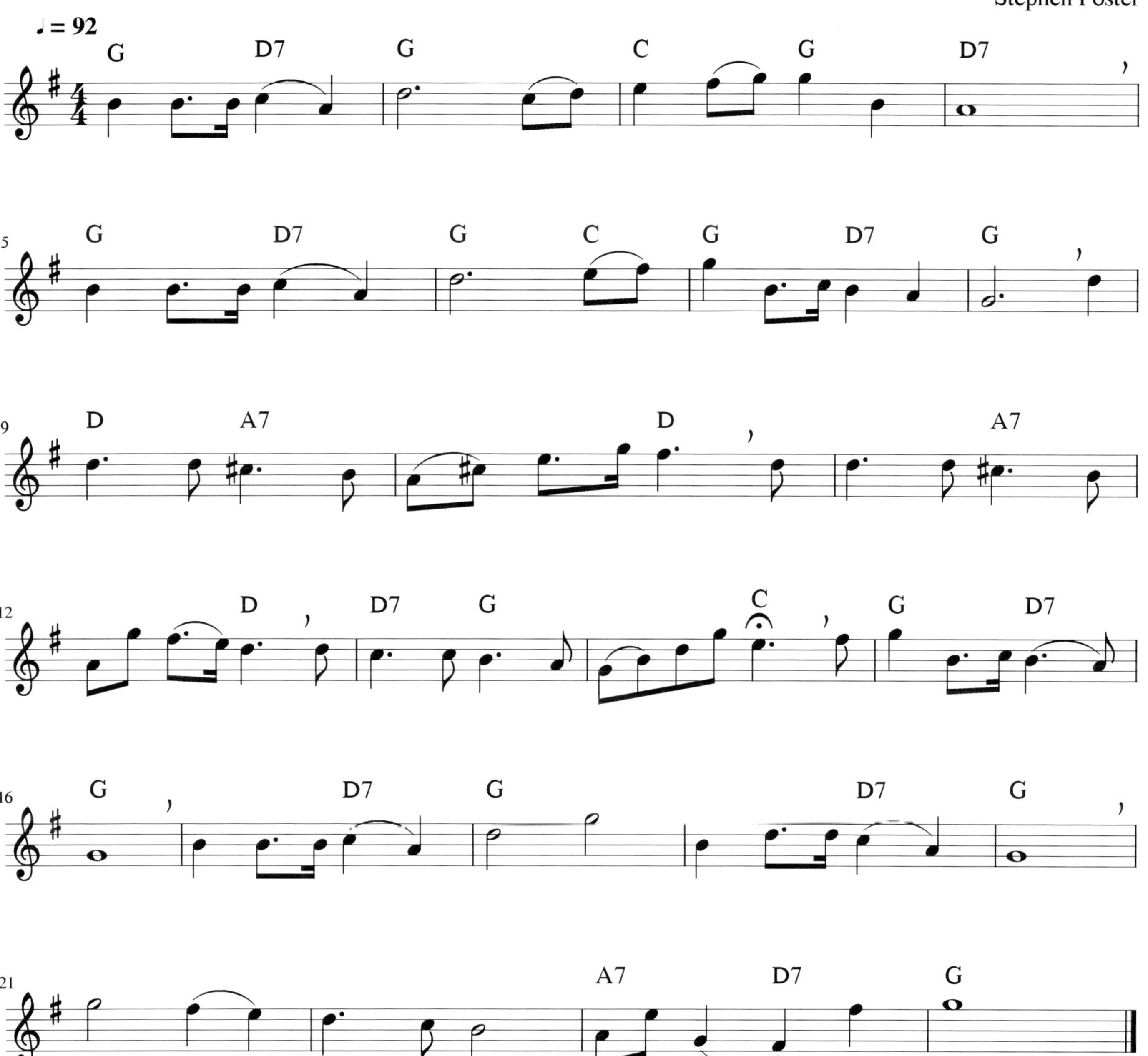

Jeanie with the Light Brown Hair

Stephen Foster

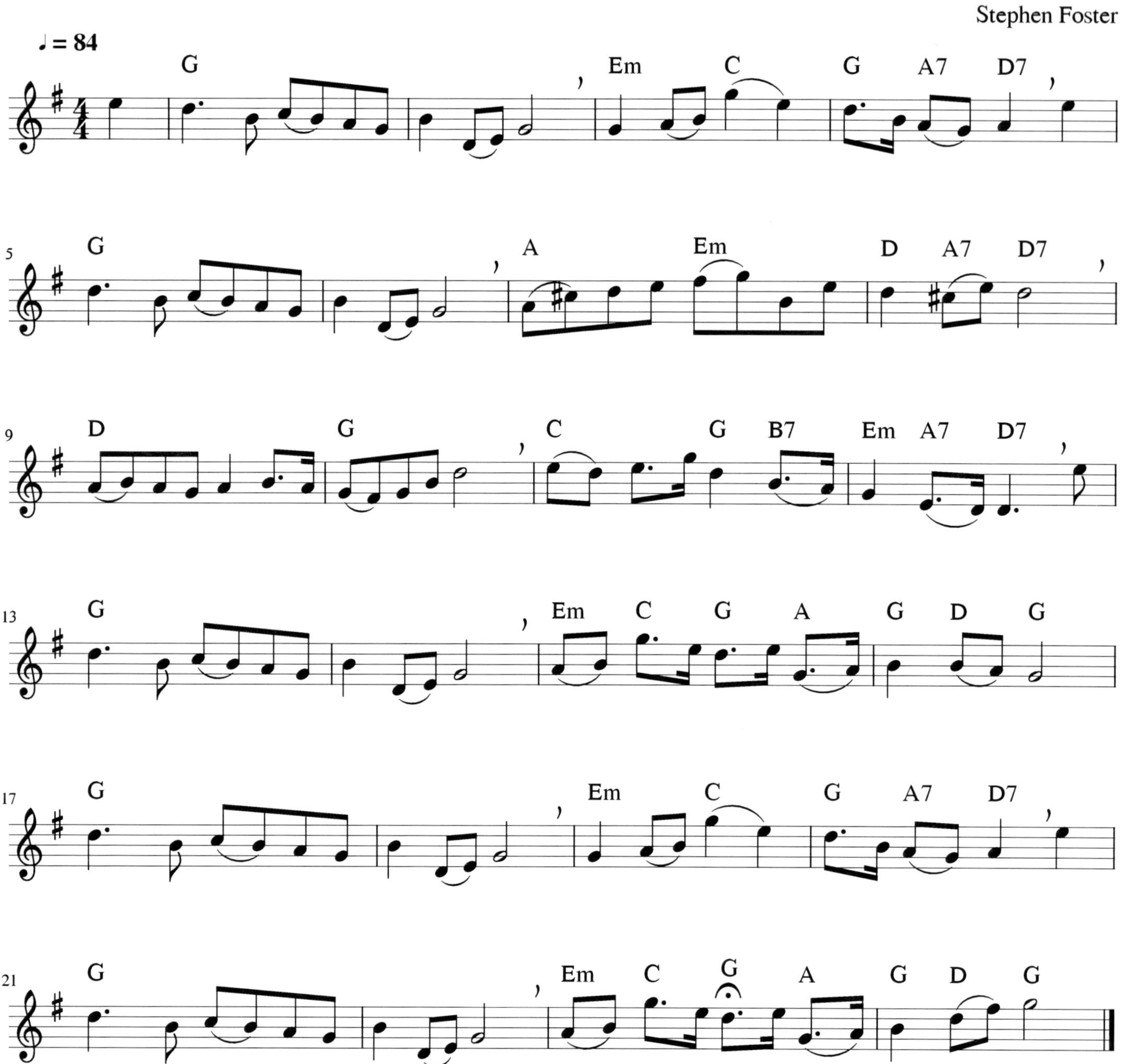

Gentle Annie

Stephen Foster

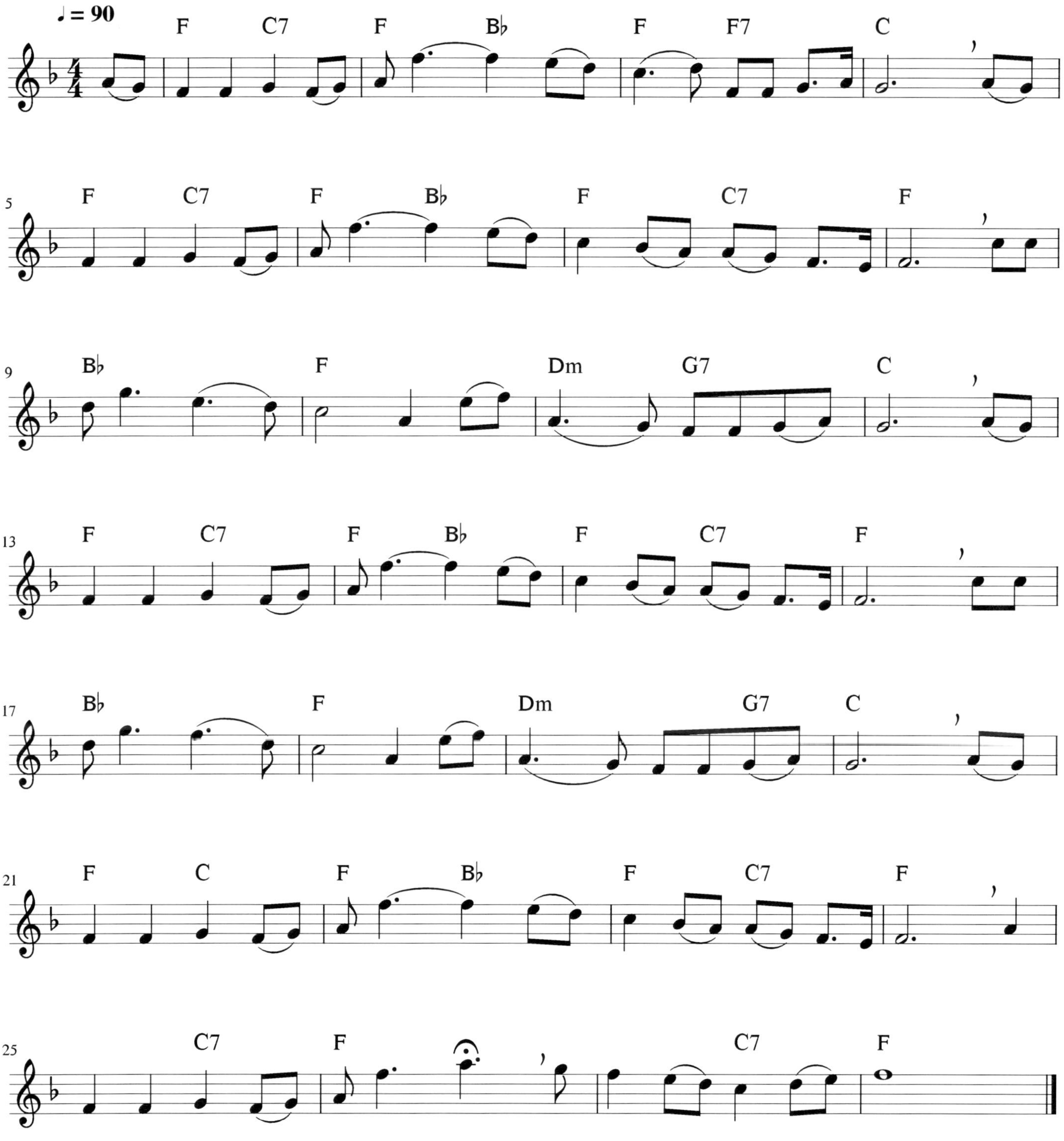

♩ = 90

F C7 F B♭ F F7 C

5 F C7 F B♭ F C7 F

9 B♭ F Dm G7 C

13 F C7 F B♭ F C7 F

17 B♭ F Dm G7 C

21 F C F B♭ F C7 F

25 C7 F C7 F

Ah! May the Red Rose Live Alway!

Stephen Foster

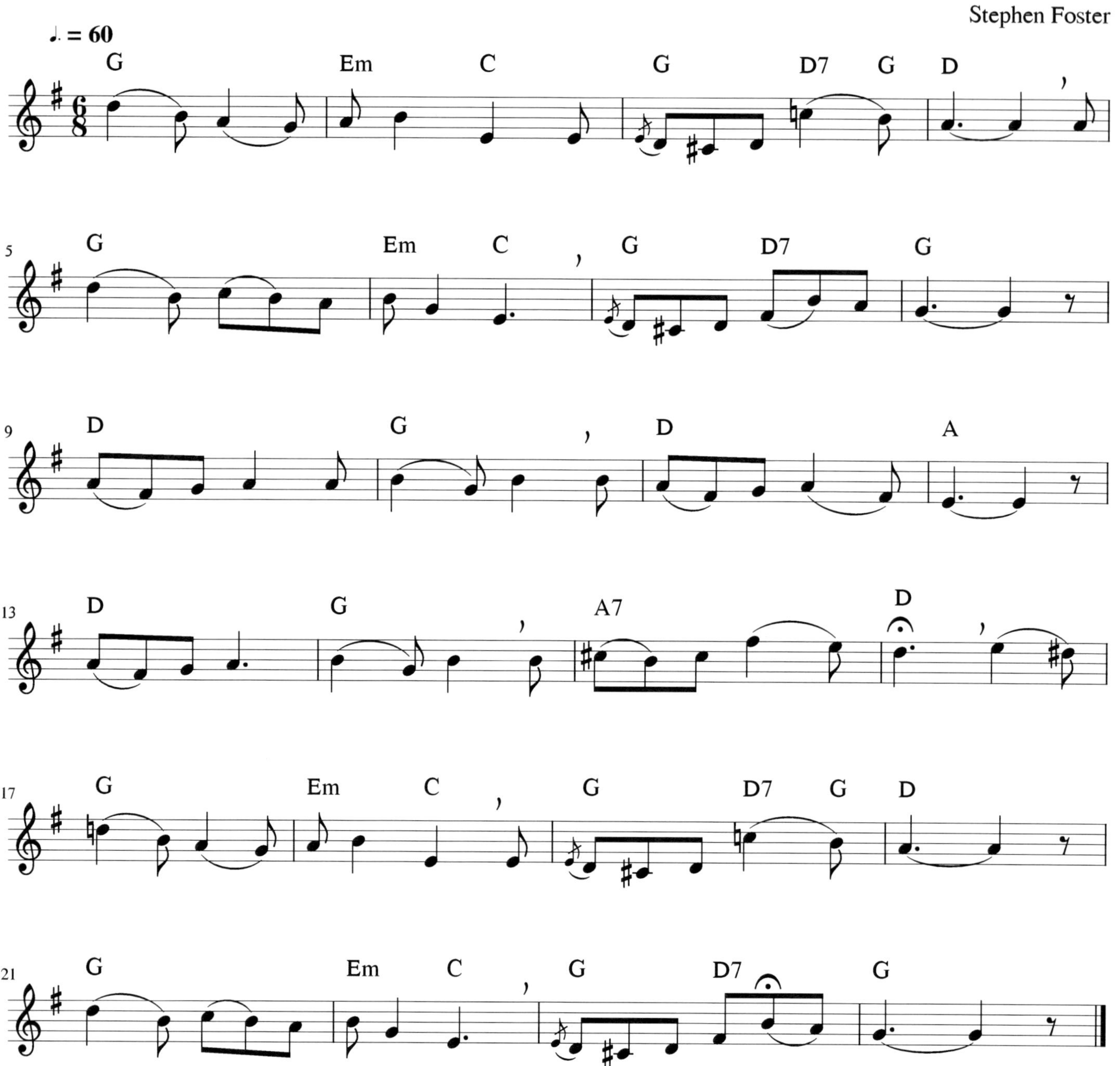

Beautiful Dreamer

Stephen Foster

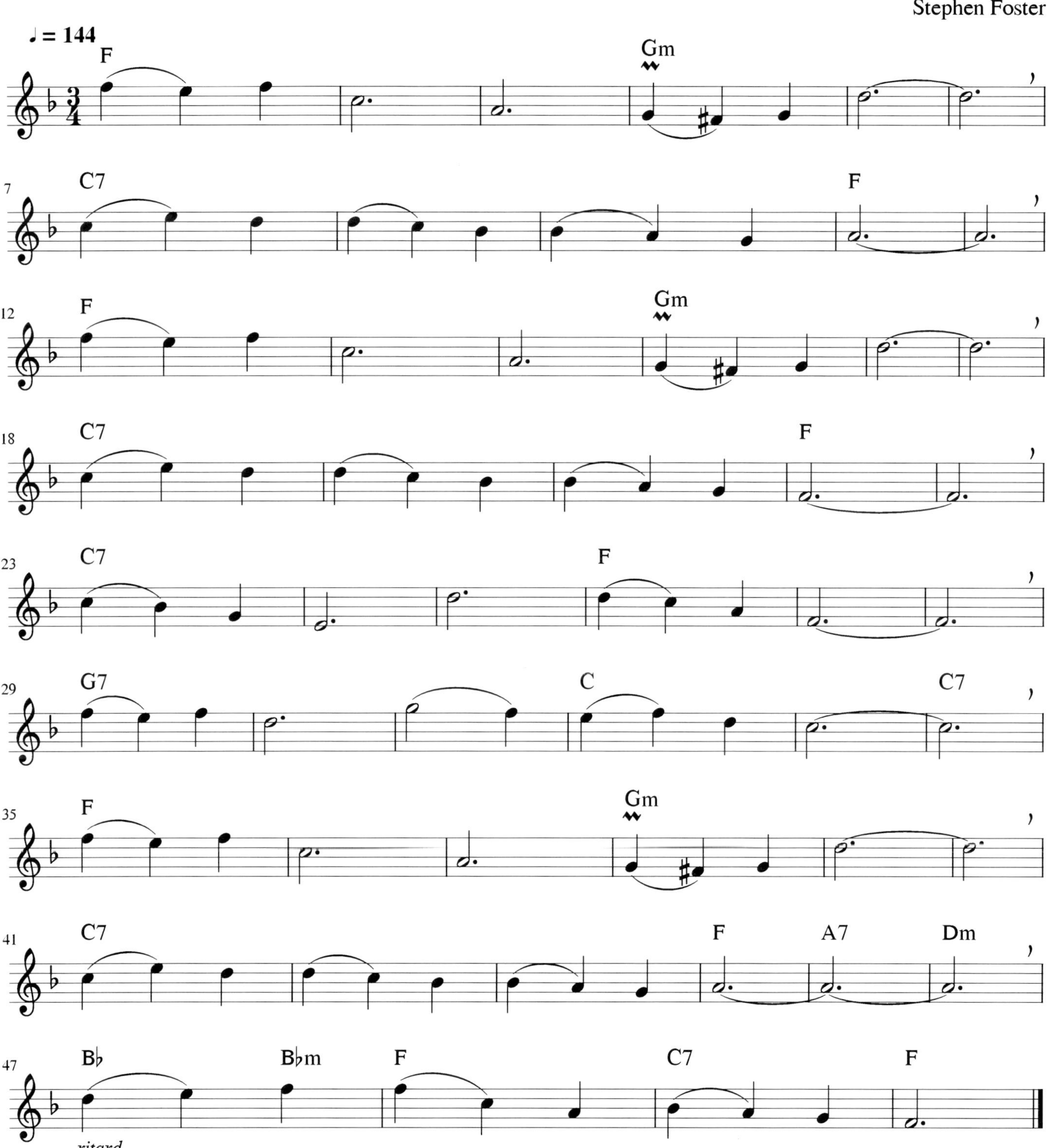

Simple Gifts

Joseph Brackett, Jr.

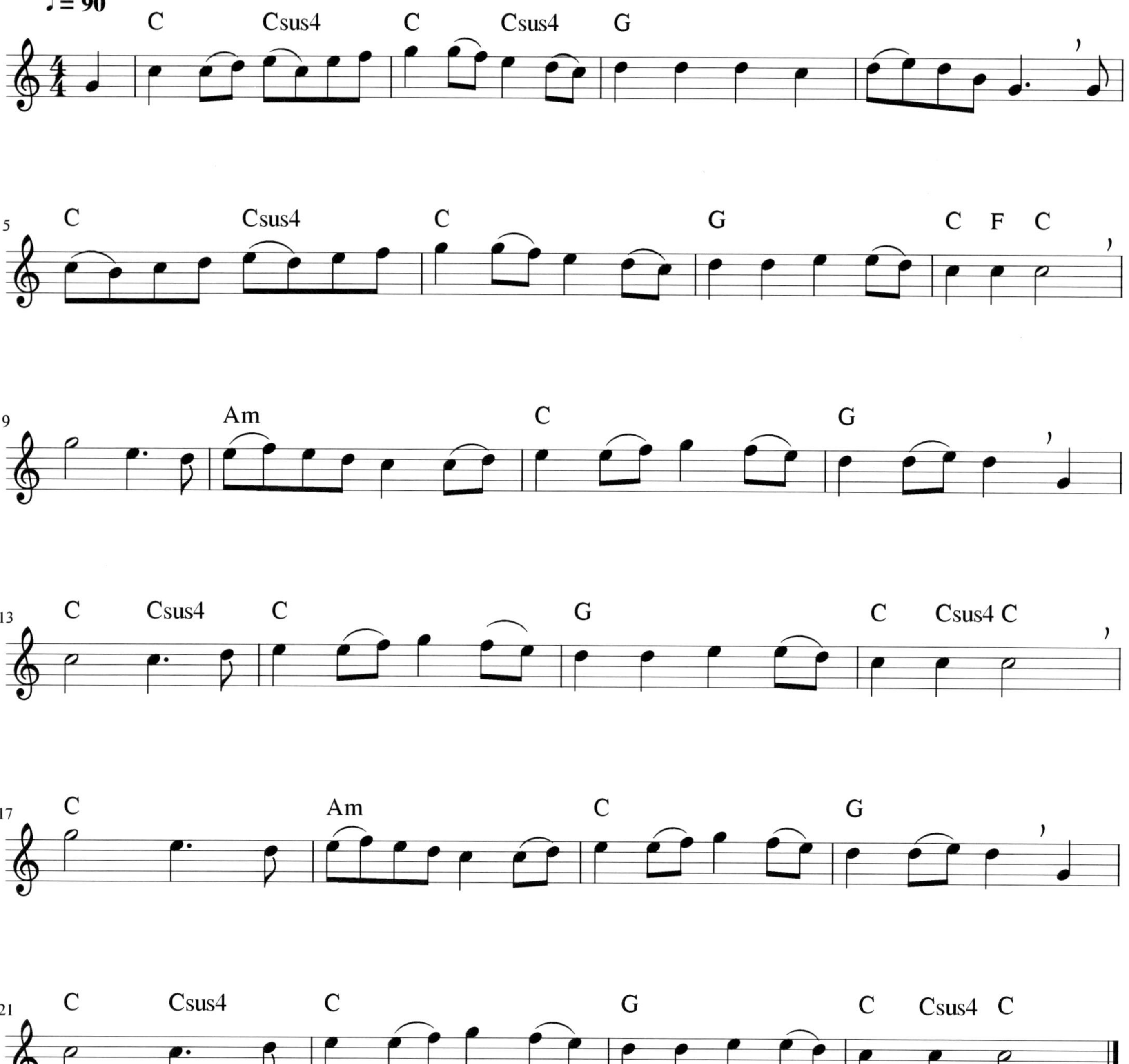

Rock Me to Sleep in the Rockies

Waltz Ballad

Gene Close

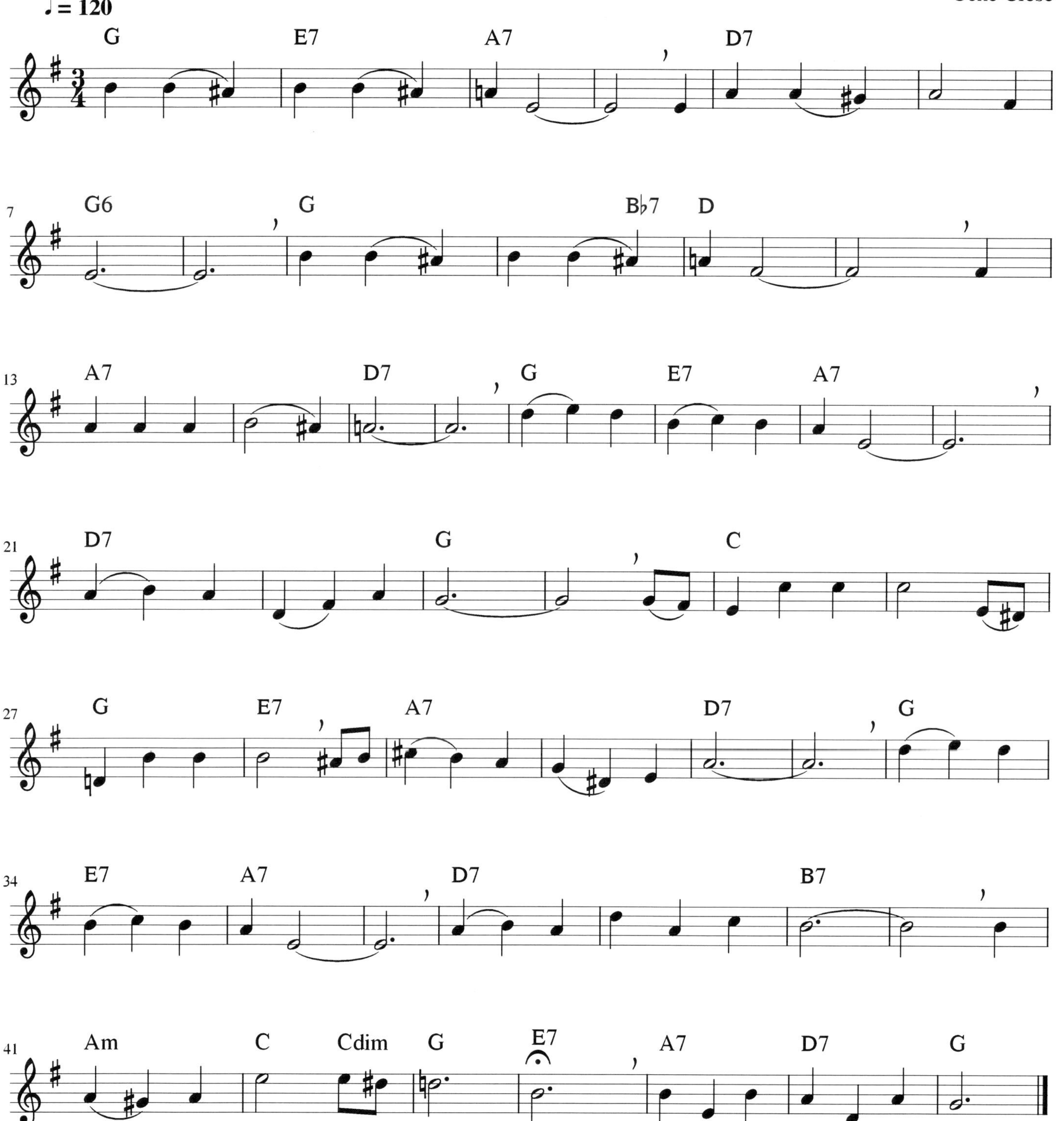

Johnny Has Gone for a Soldier

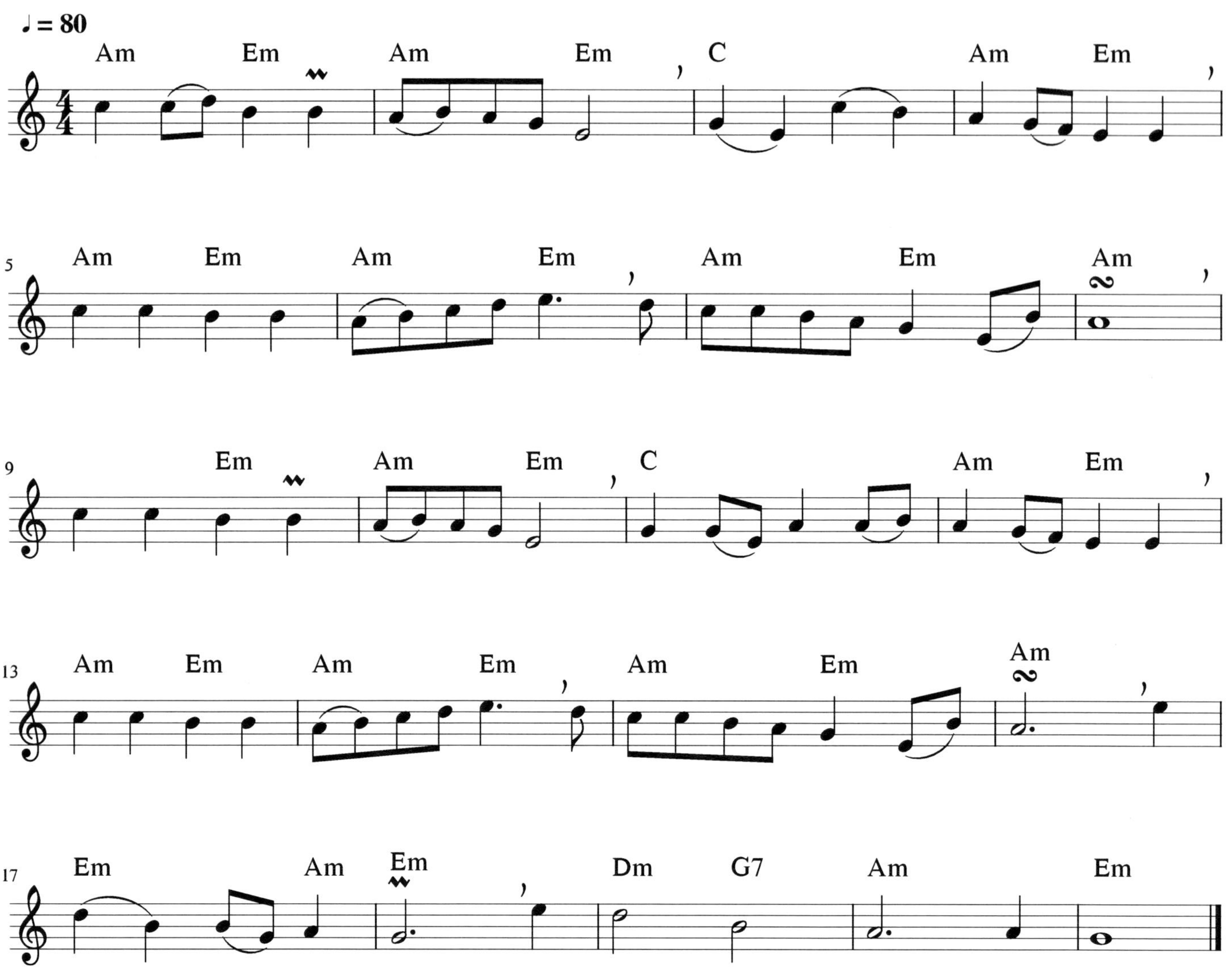

Oh, Bury Me Beneath the Old Willow

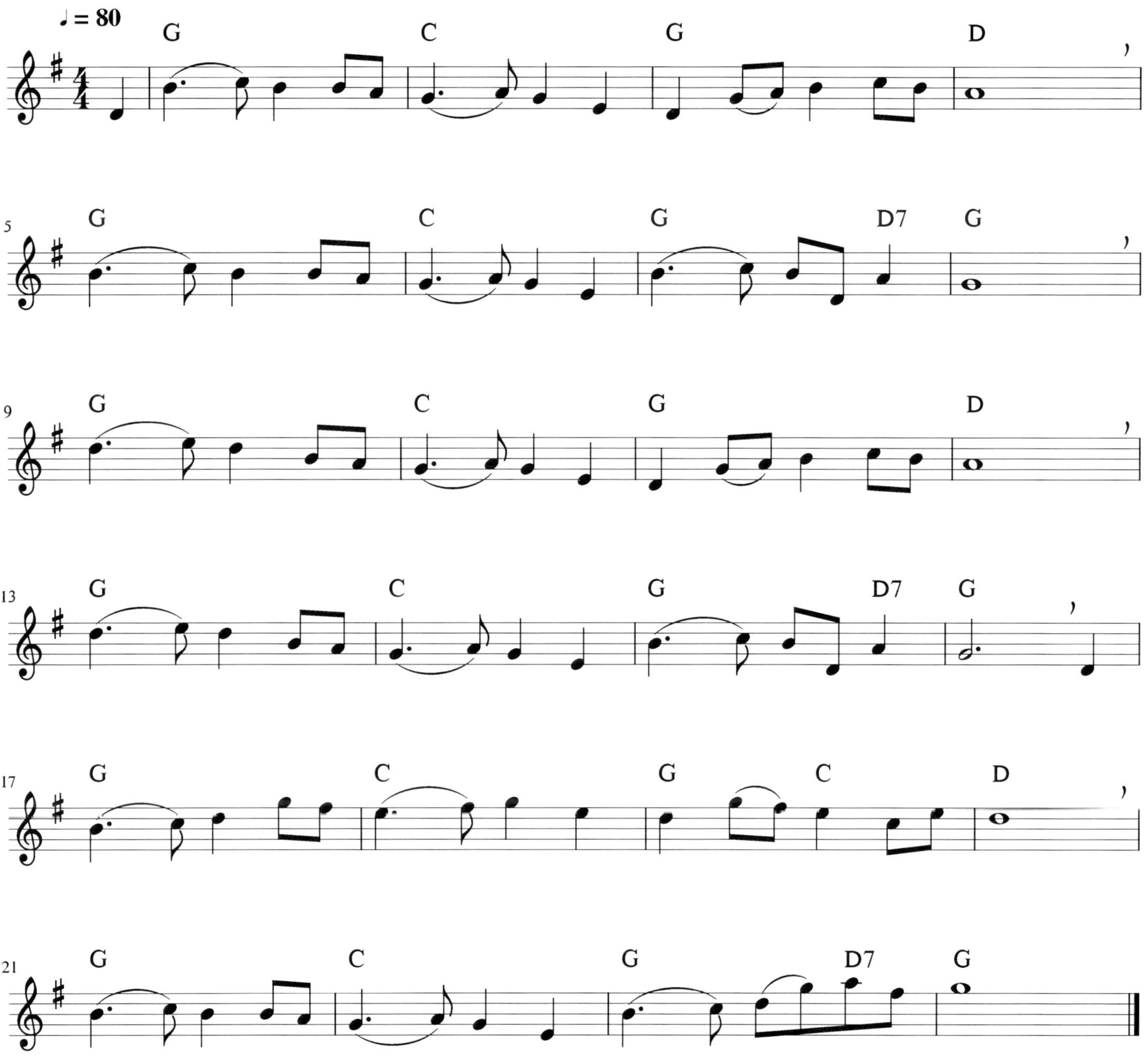

Darling Nelly Gray

B. R. Hanby

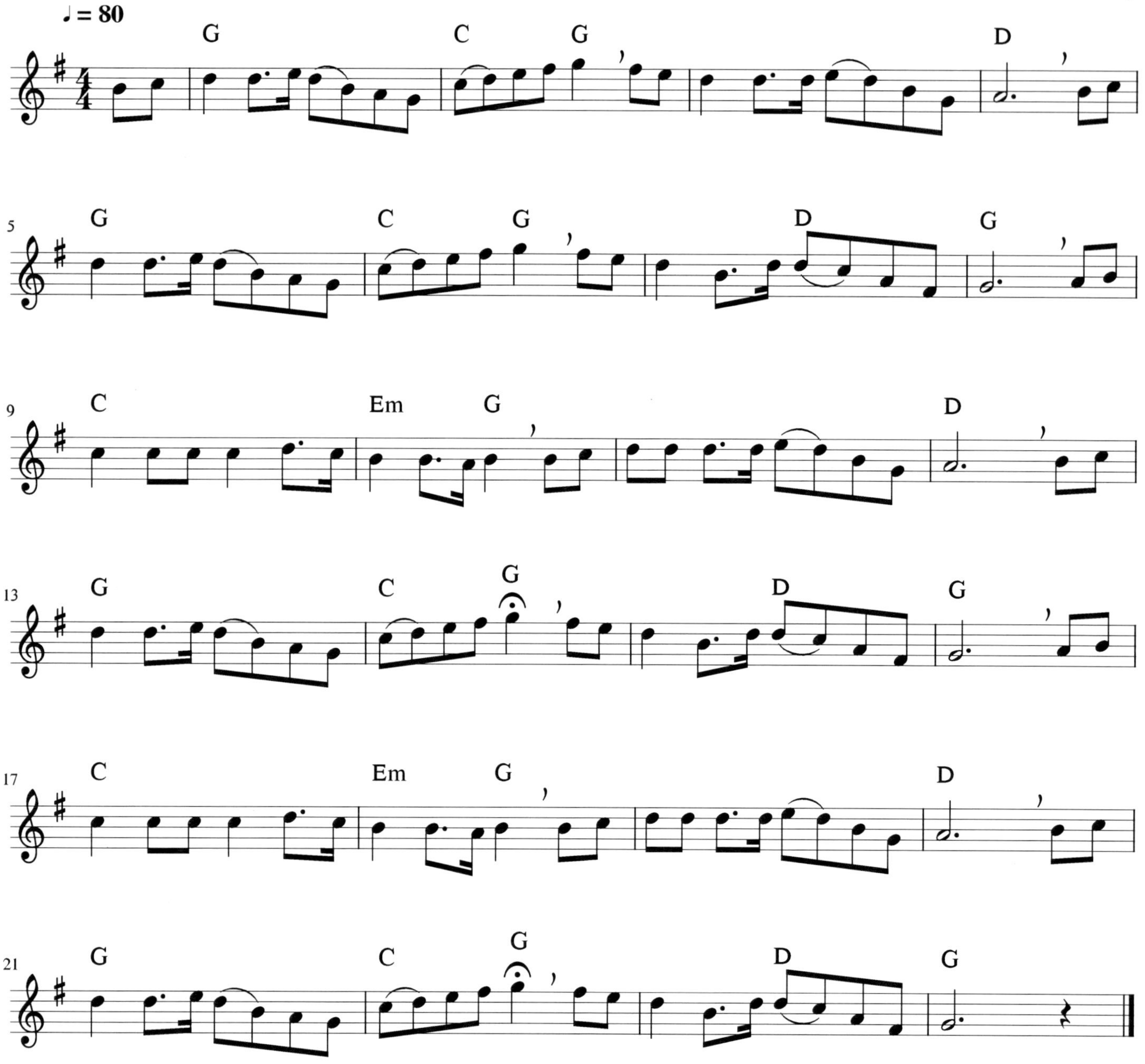

♩ = 80

G C G D

5 G C G D G

9 C Em G D

13 G C G D G

17 C Em G D

21 G C G D G

I Never Will Marry

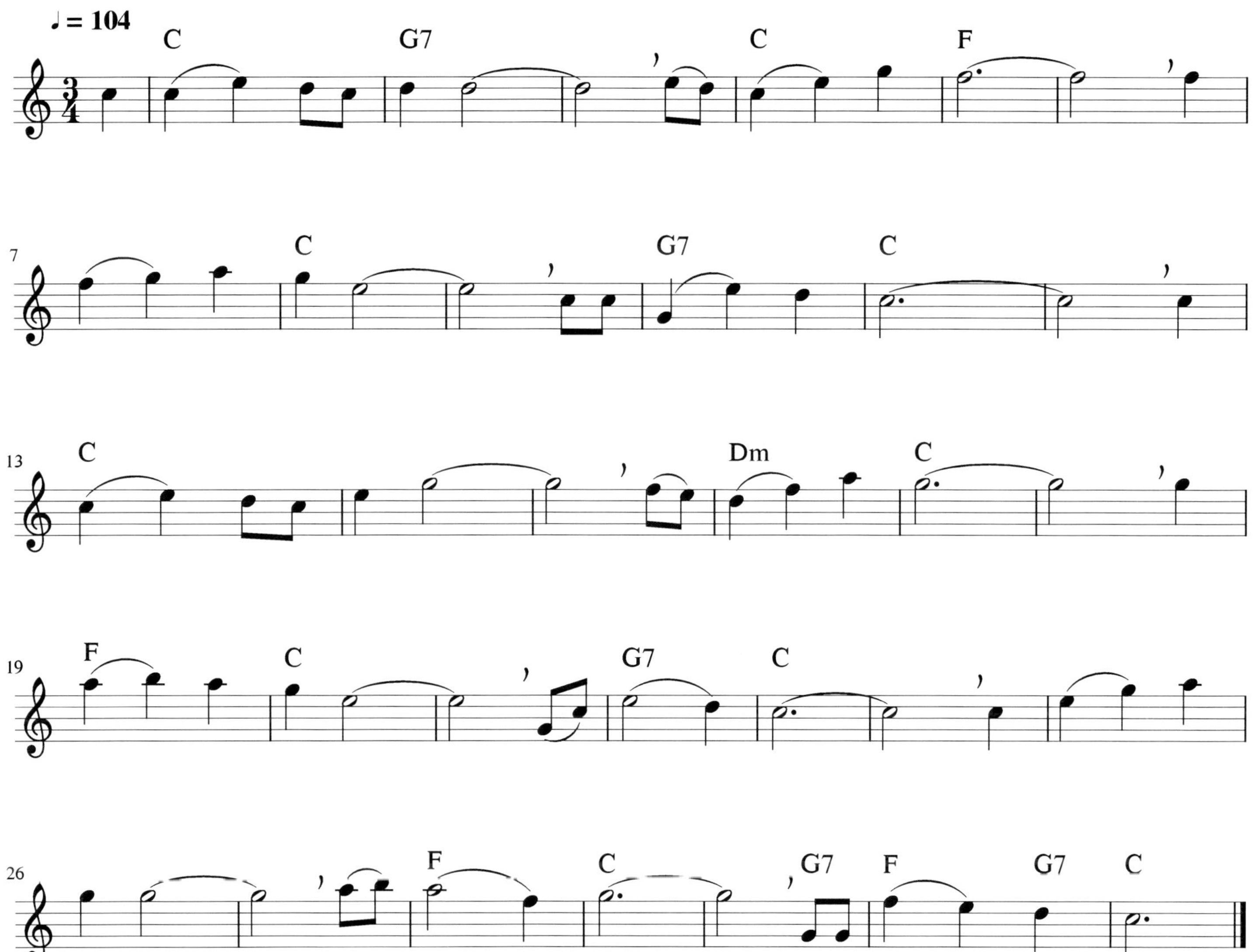

When You and I Were Young, Maggie

J. A. Butterfield

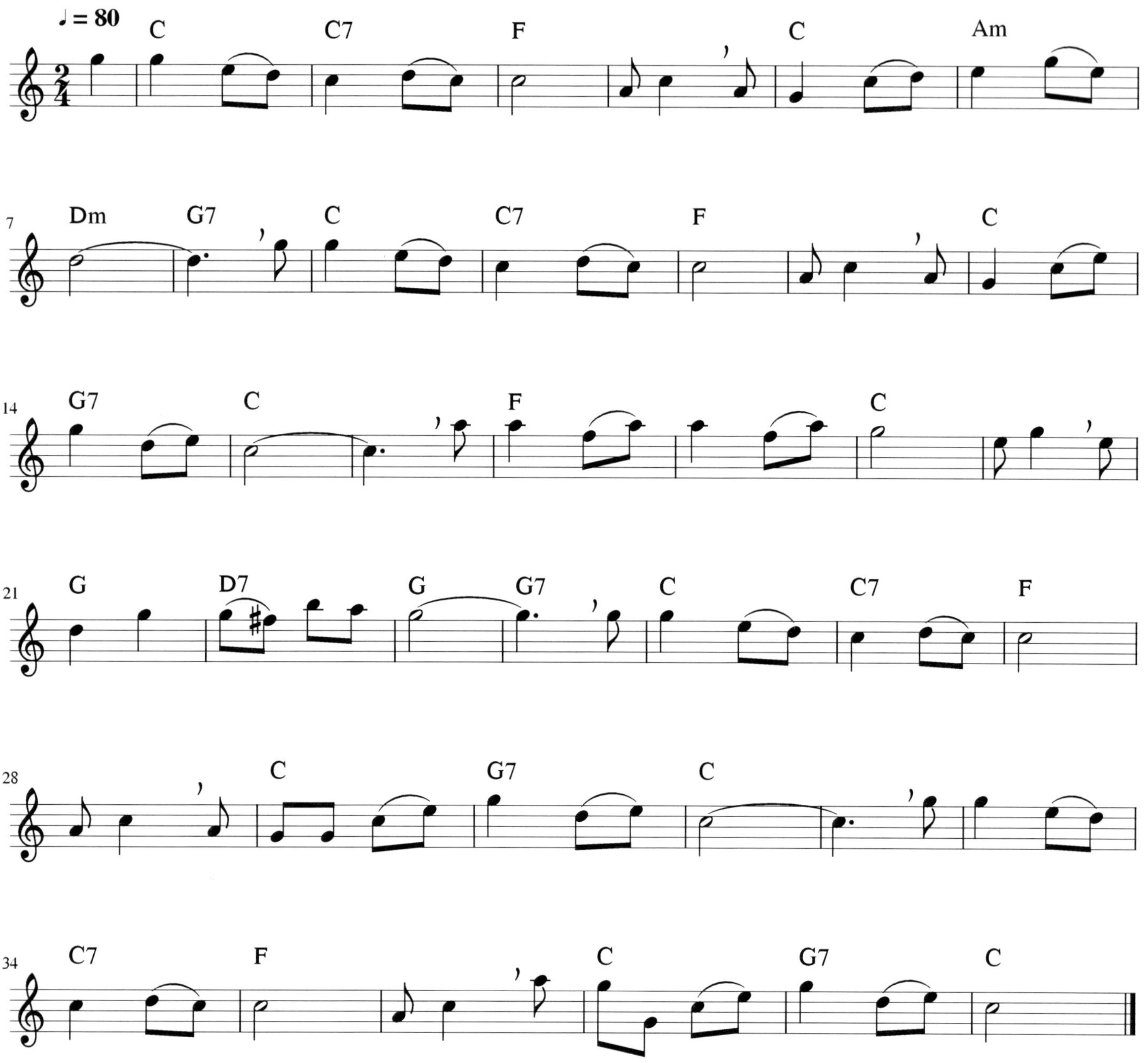

♩ = 80

Mighty Like a Rose

Ethelbert Nevin

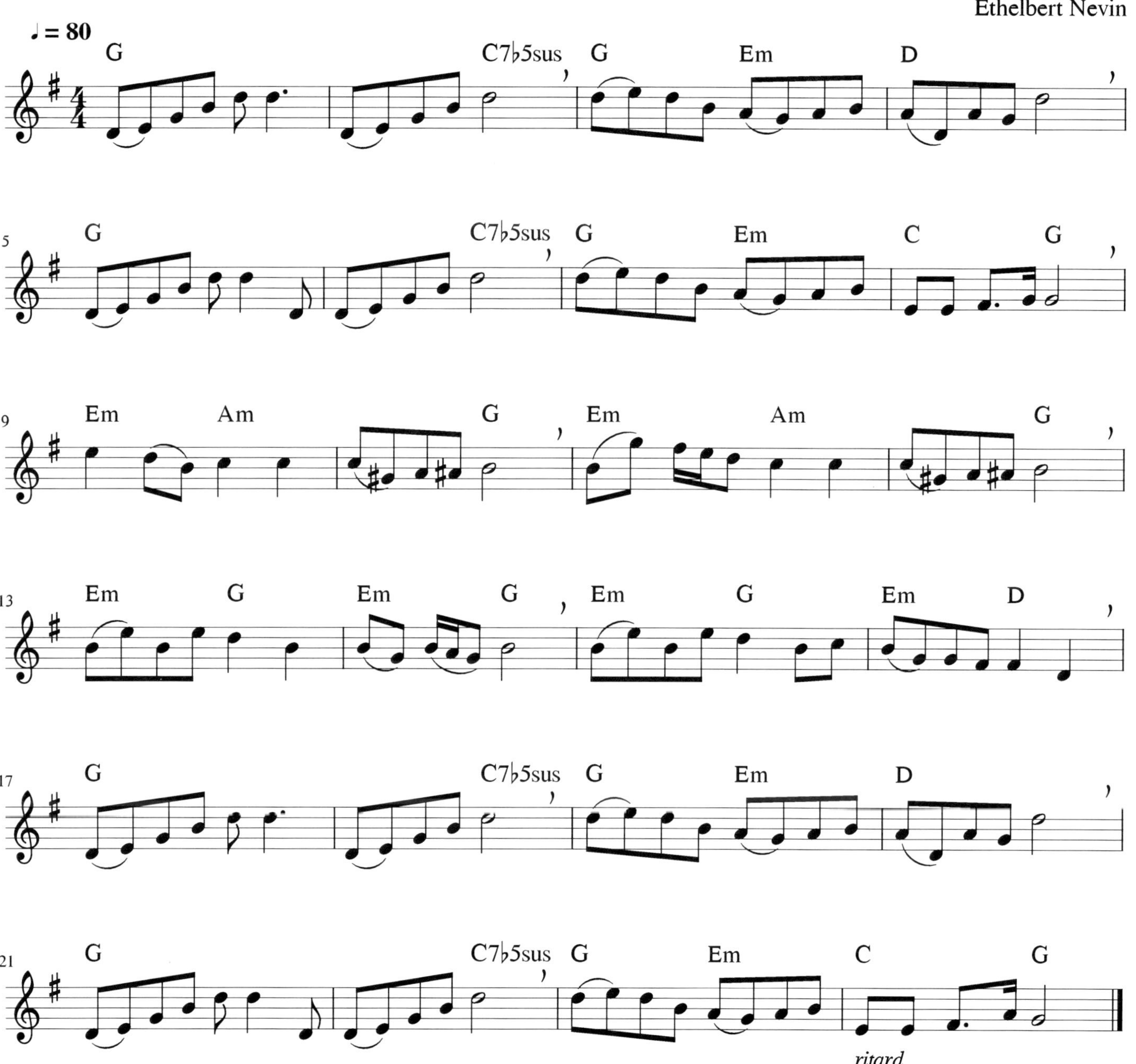

To a Wild Rose

Edward MacDowell

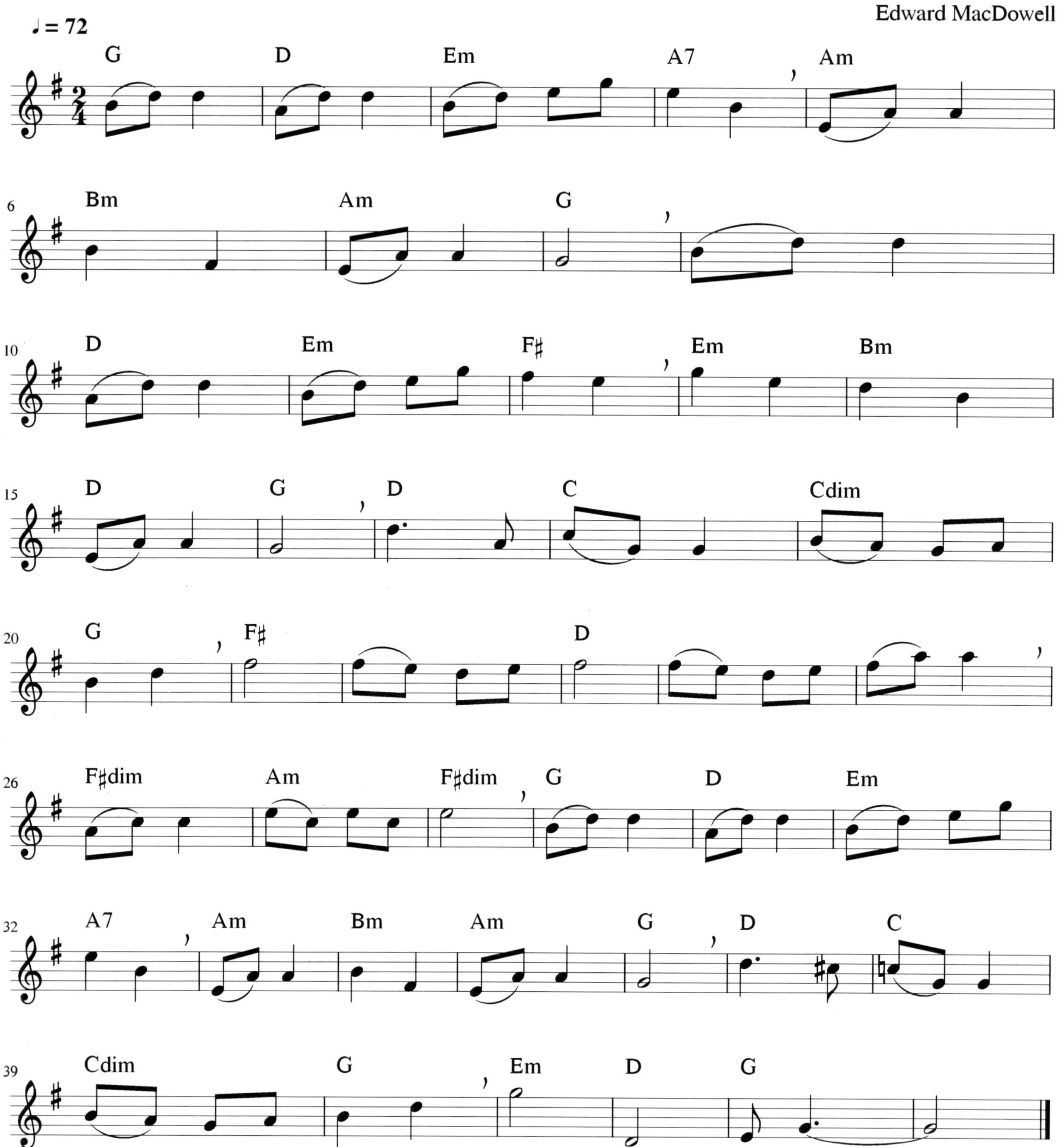

Wayfaring Stranger

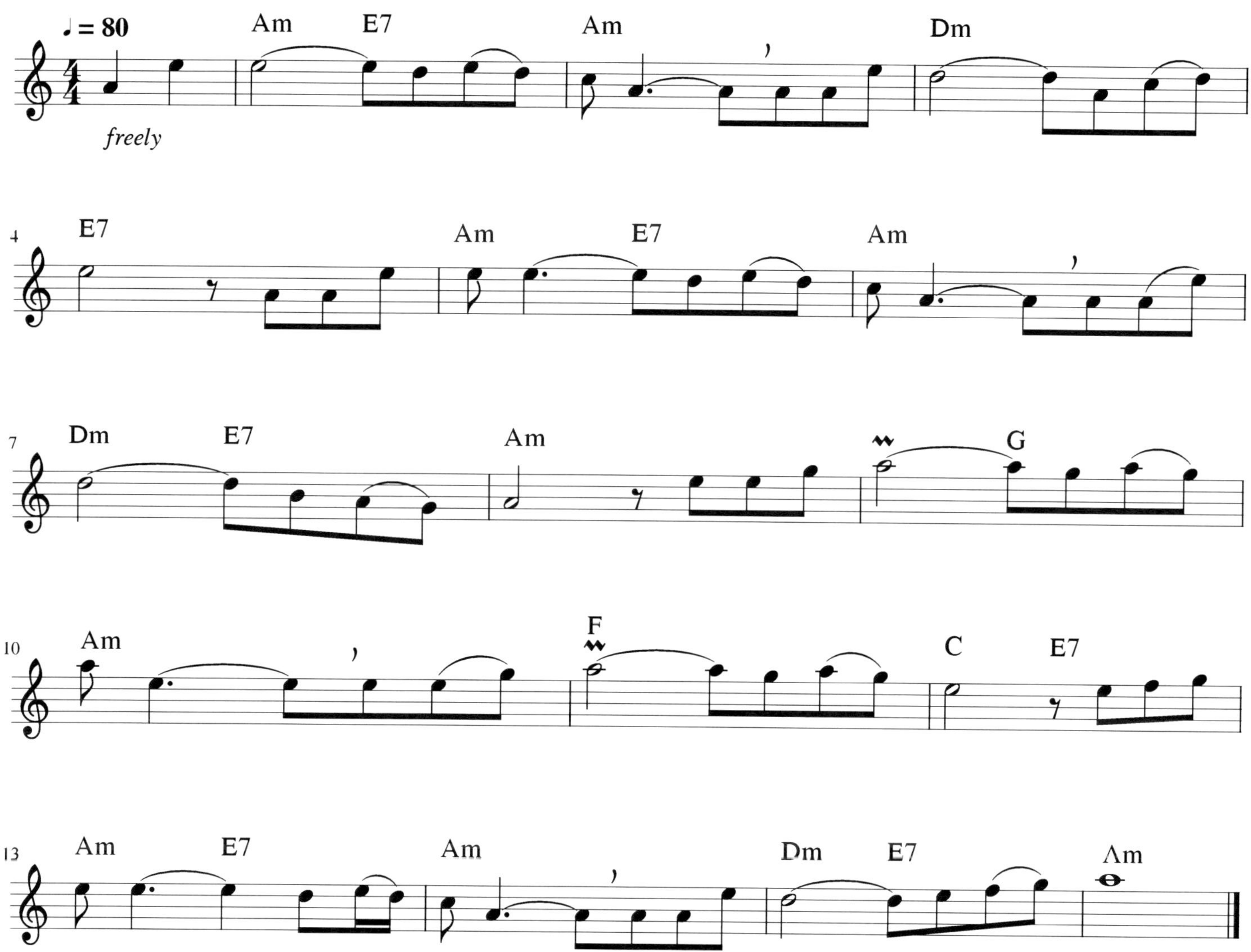

Sunset in the Hills

Waltz Ballad

Norman Hedges

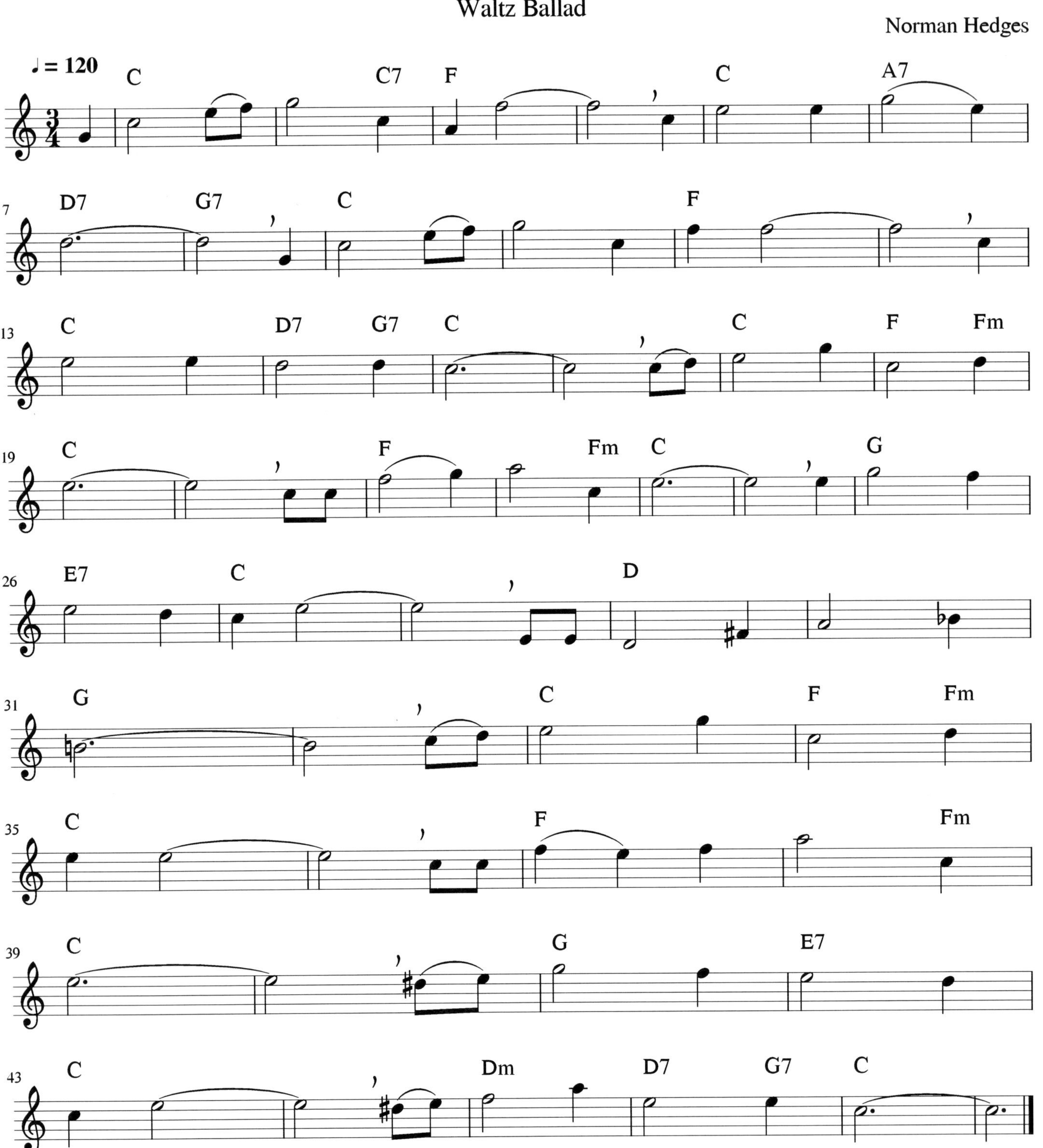

The Last Request

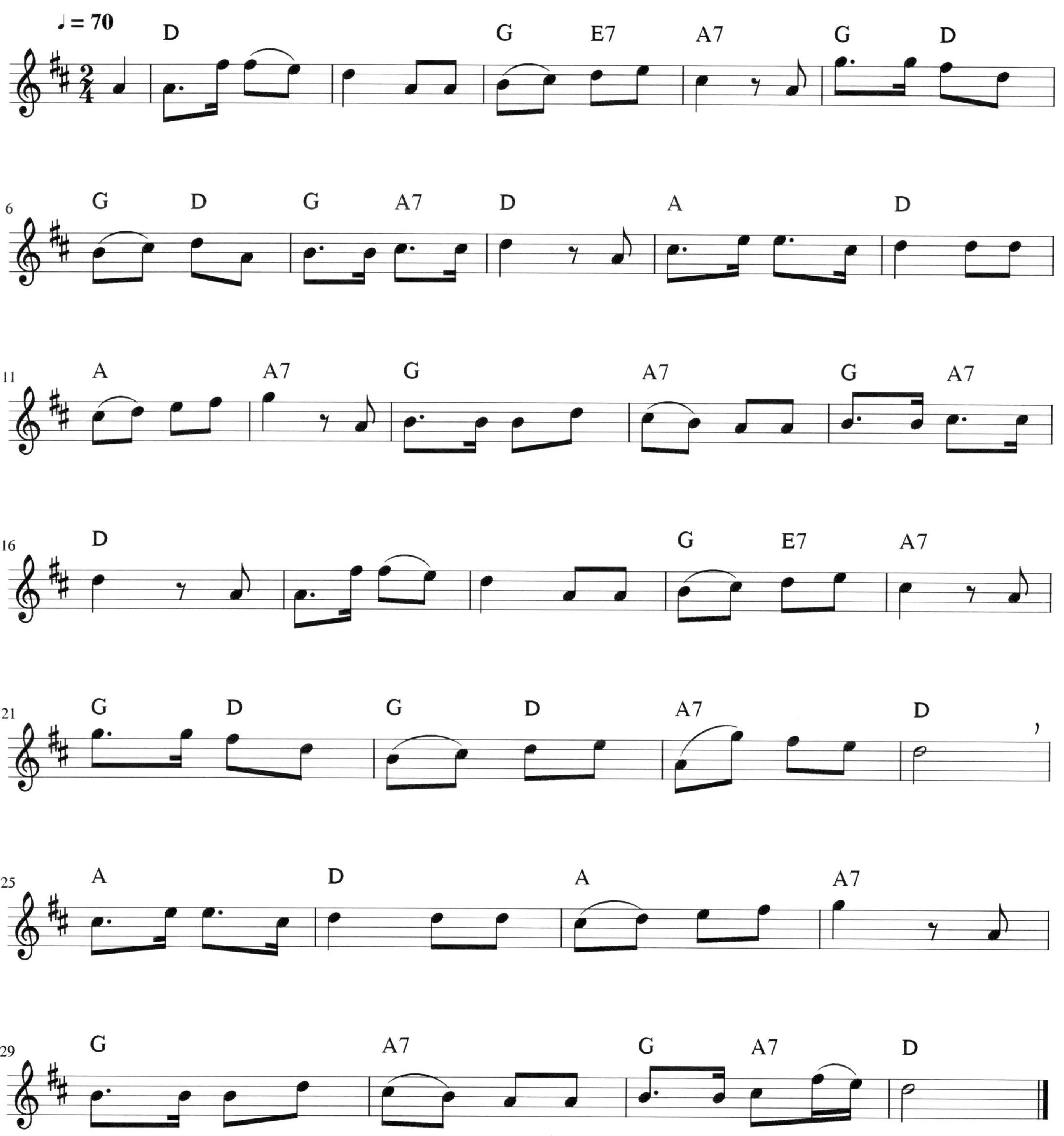

Lorena

J. P. Webster

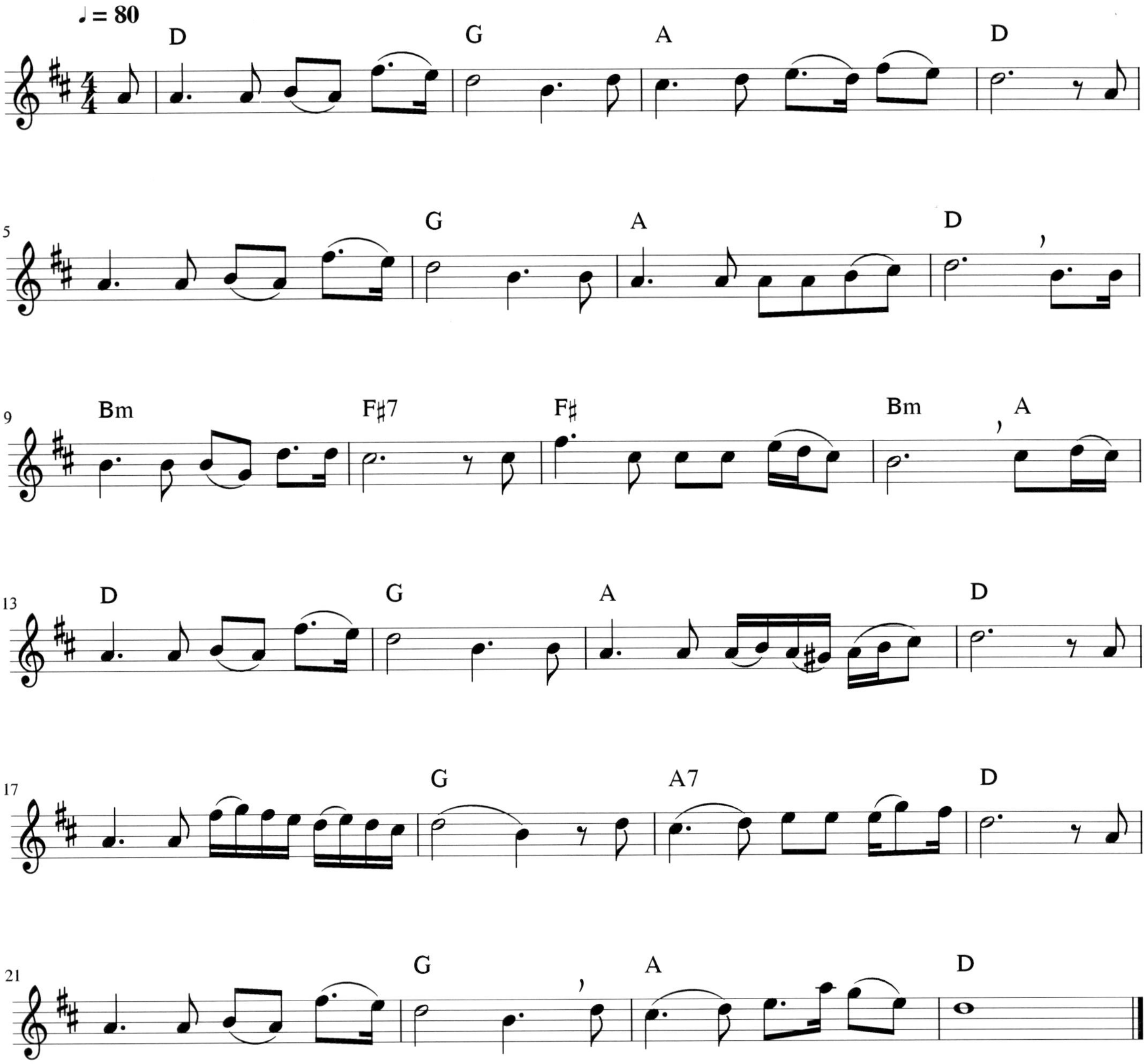

♩ = 80

D G A D

5 G A D

9 Bm F♯7 F♯ Bm A

13 D G A D

17 G A7 D

21 G A D

Nightingales Sing

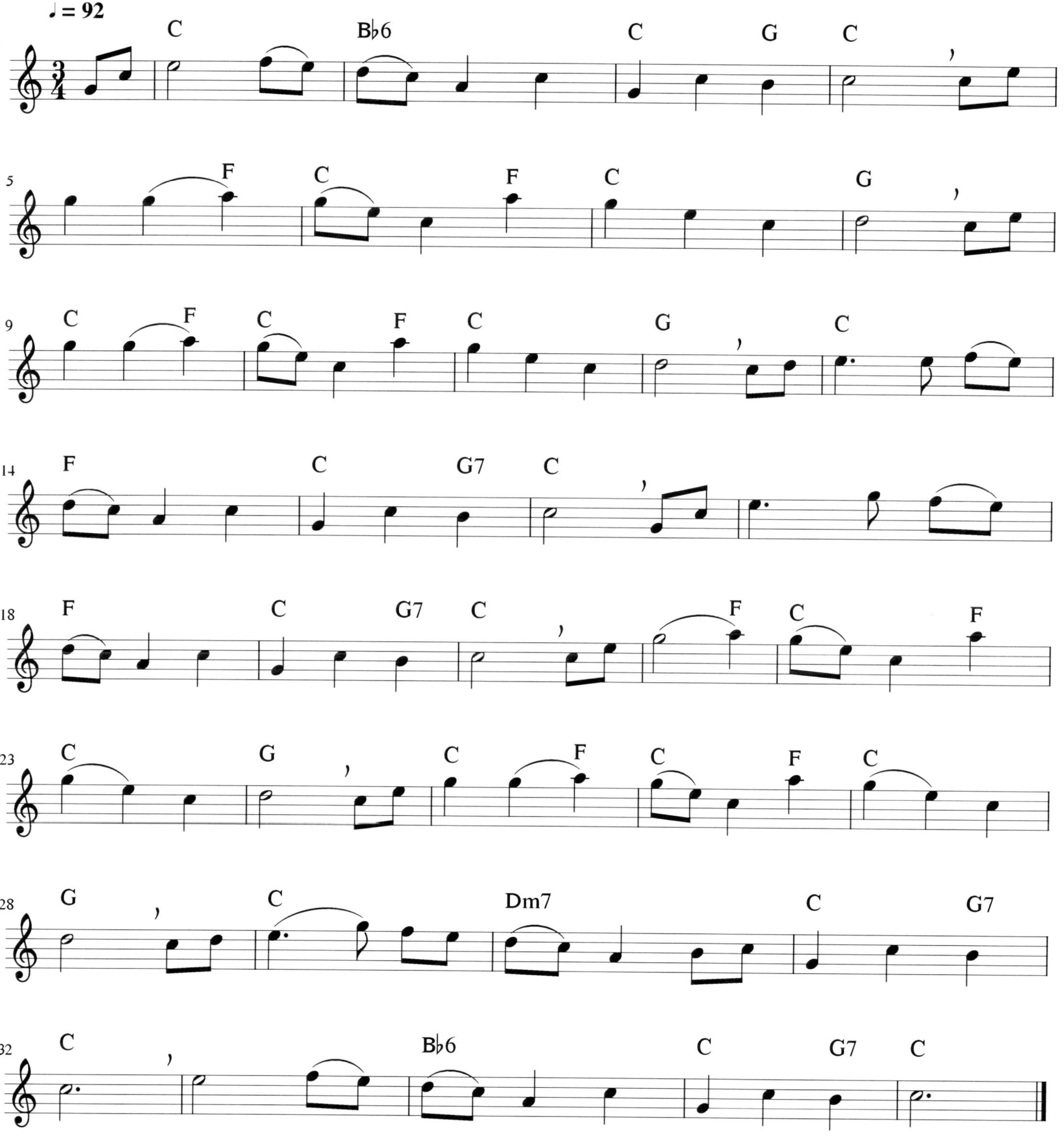

In the Pines

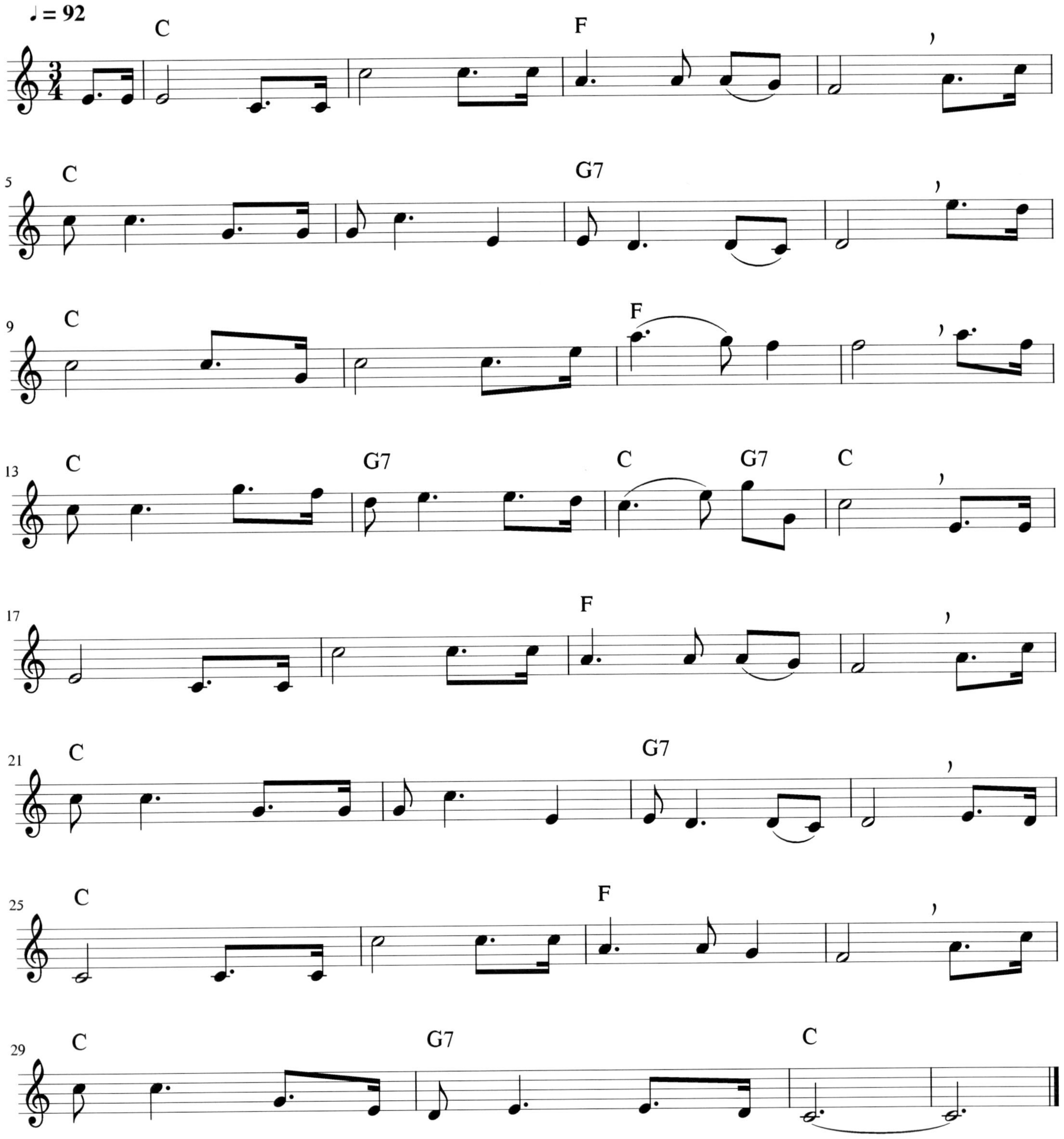

Sweet, Sweet Is Thy Face

Carl Arini

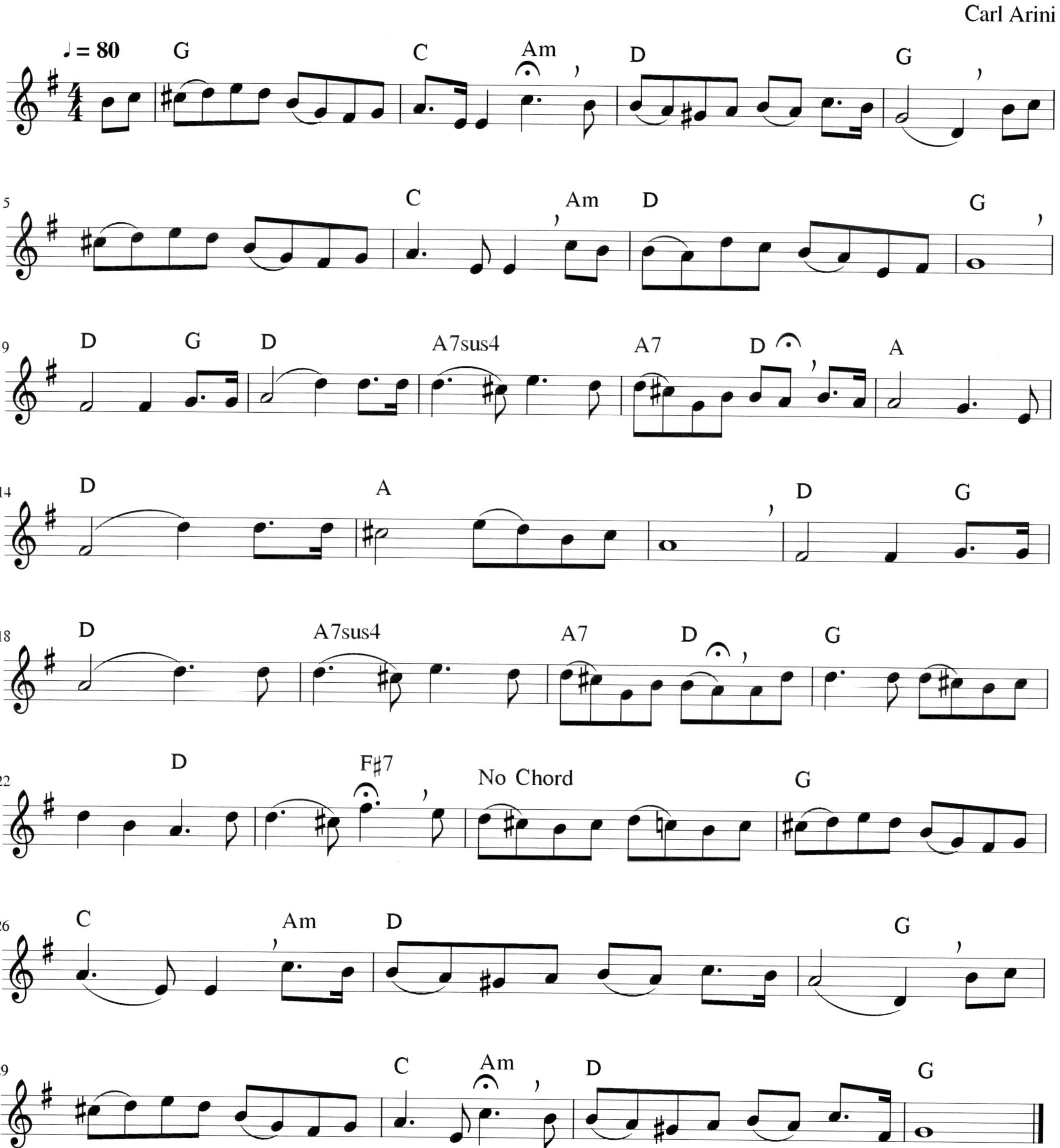

Rock Me to Sleep, Mother

John H. Hewitt

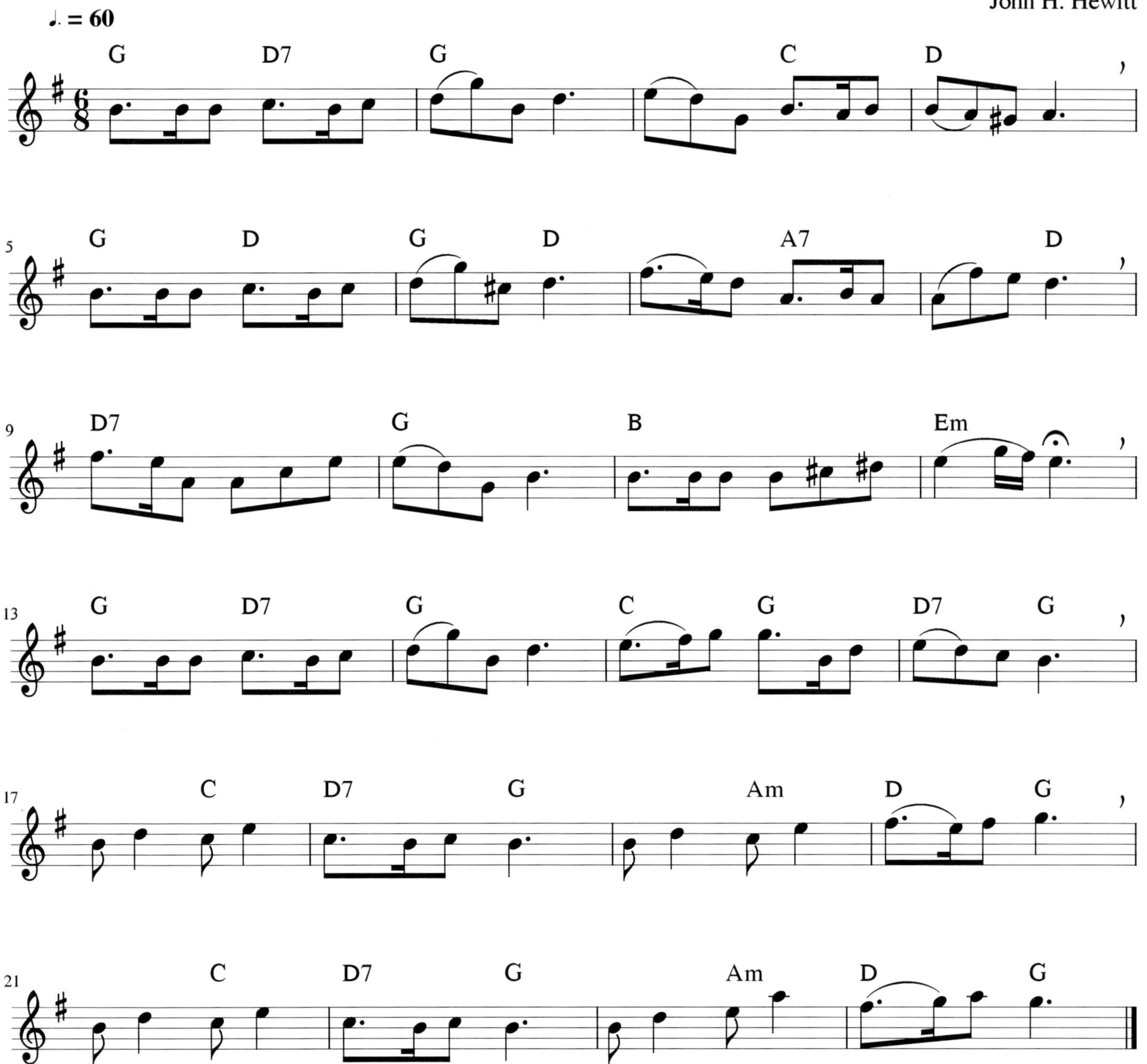

Old Nevada Home

Waltz Ballad

Billy Oudeans & Will Livernash

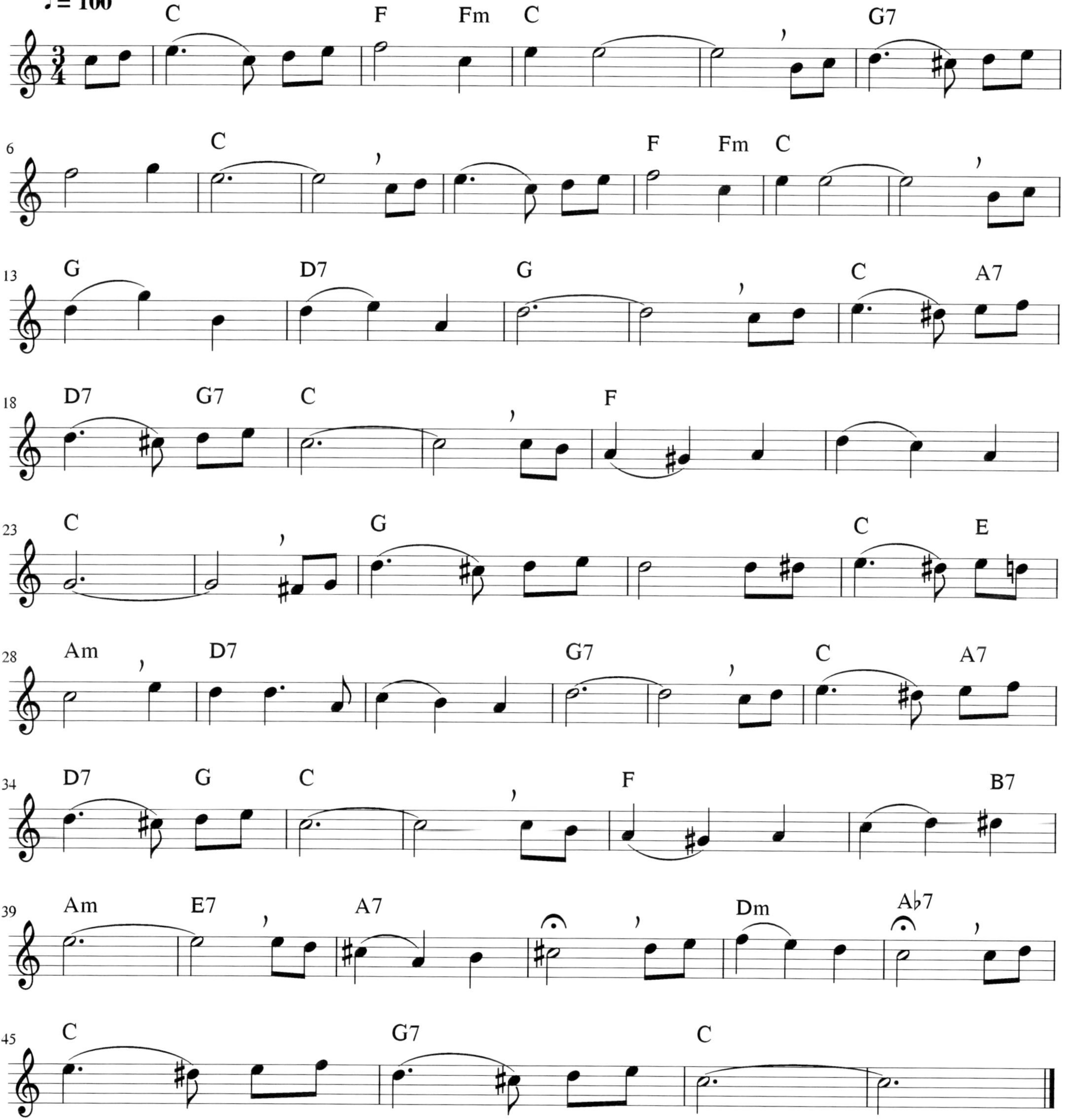

Pretty Peggy

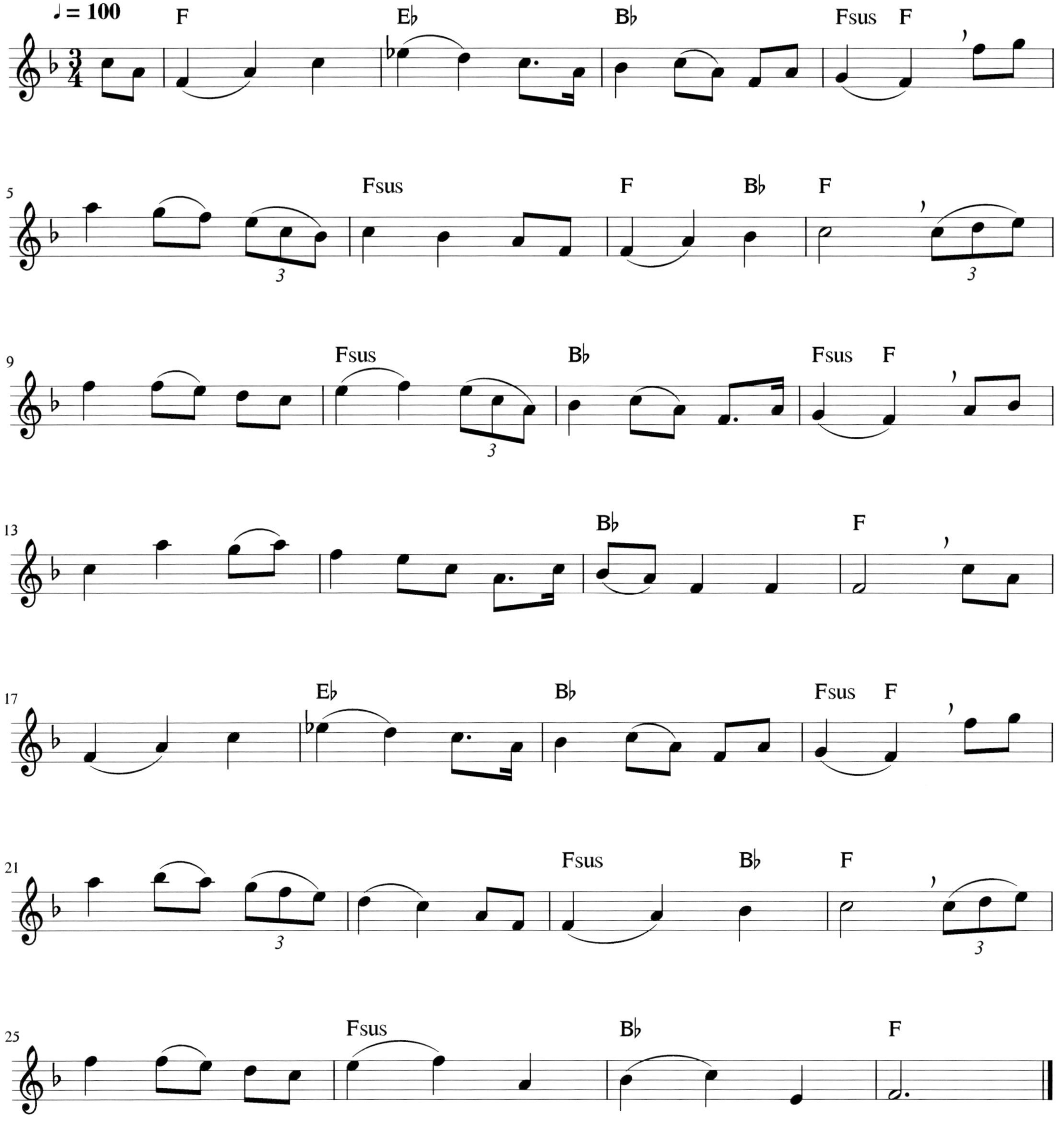

Just Before the Battle, Mother

George F. Root

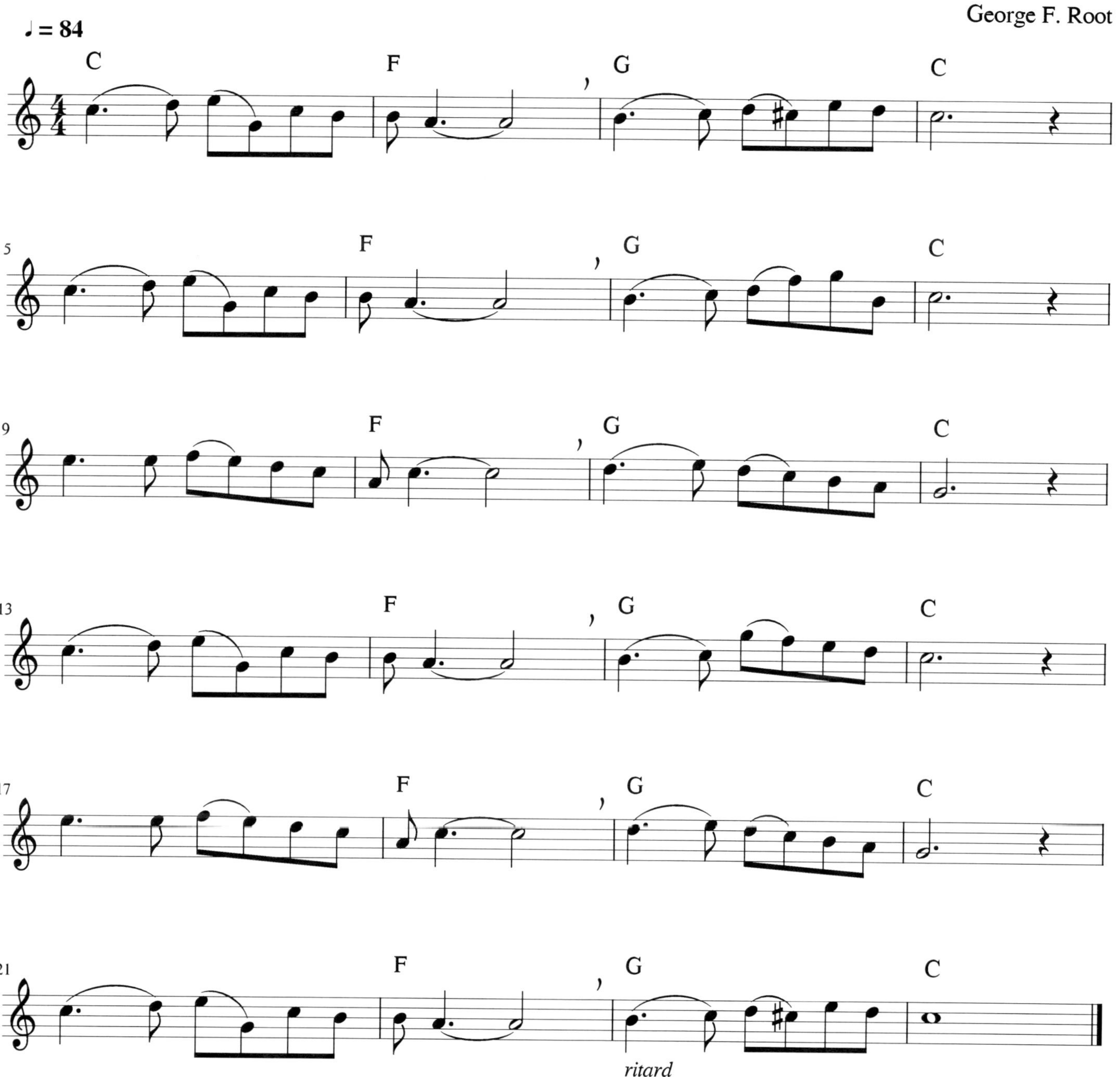

Shenandoah

♩ = 80
G C G D7 D7 G
freely
5 Em G C G Bm C
9 G D7 G D Em
13 C D7 G Em G C
17 G Bm7 C G D7 G
3

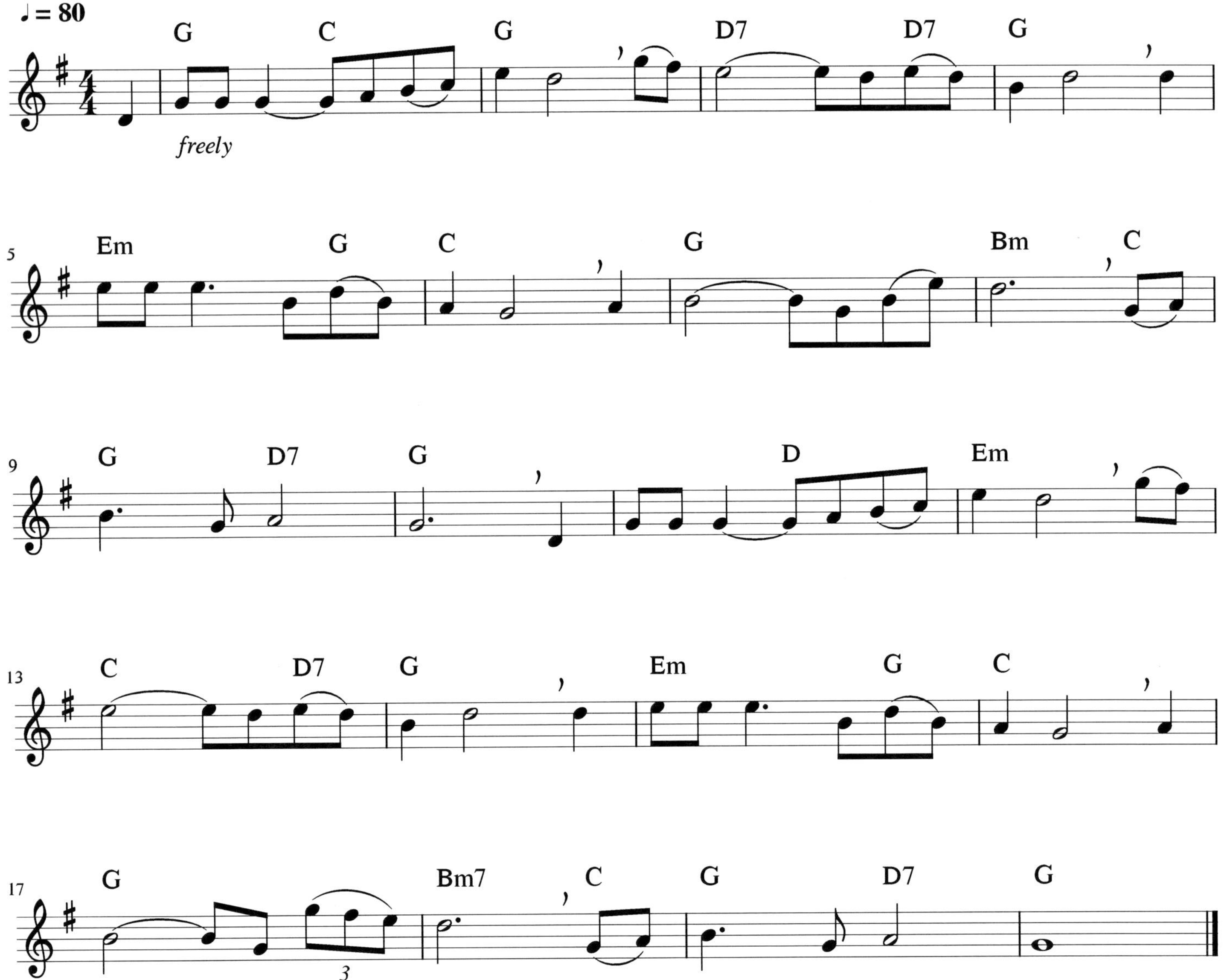

Jefferson and Liberty

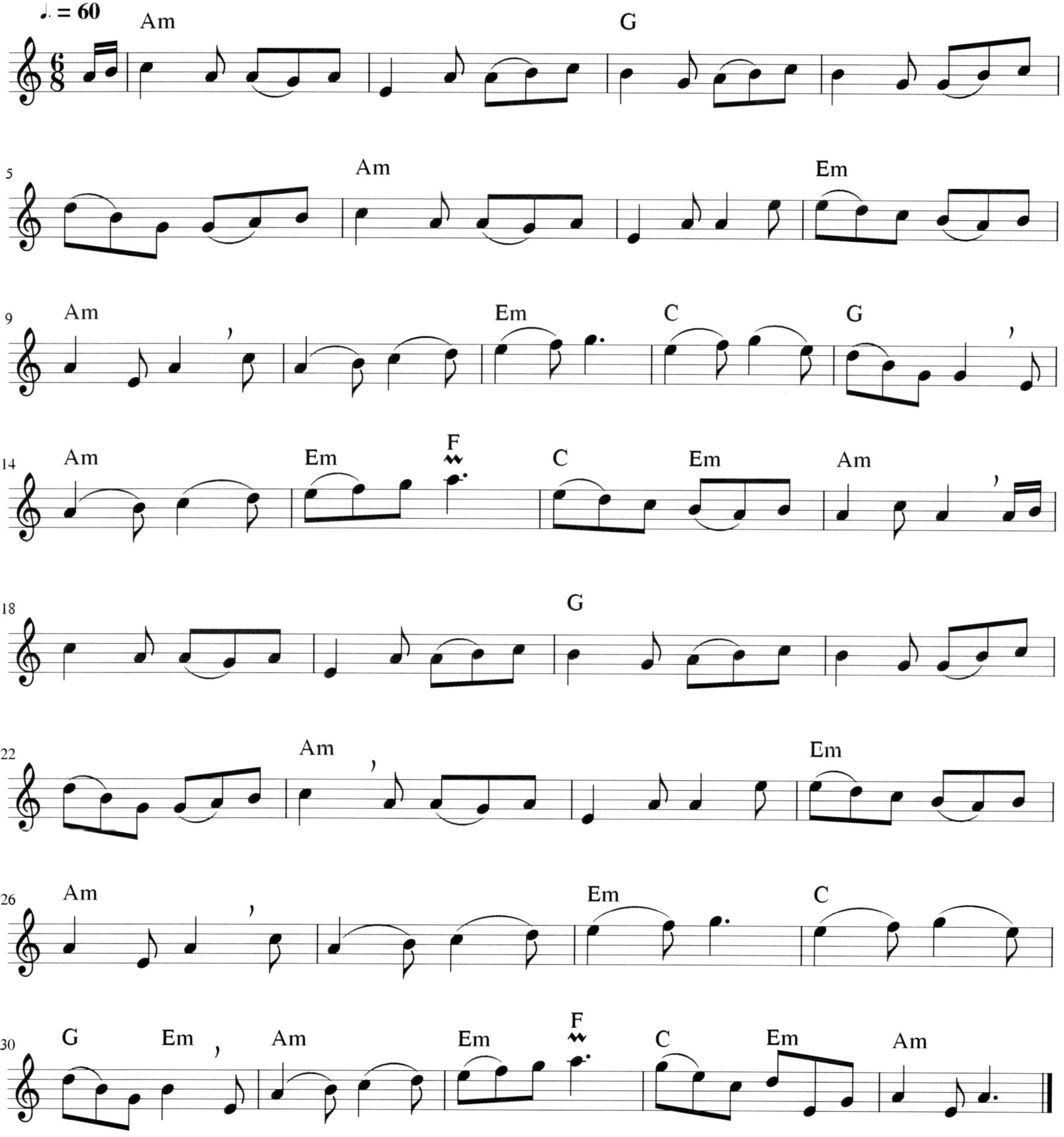

By the Sea Alone I Wander

S. P. Wardwell

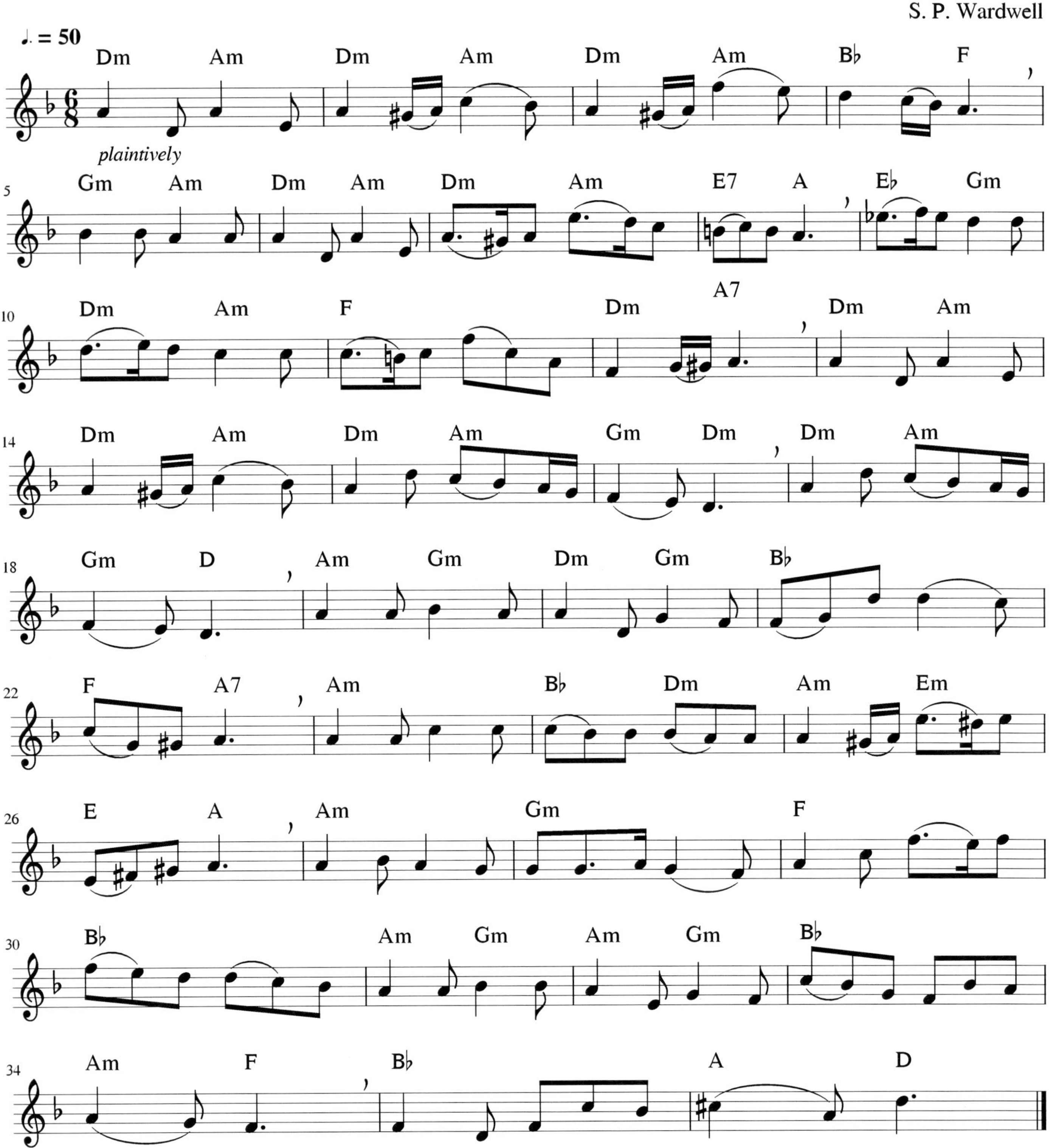

Where the Mountains Kiss the Sky

Waltz Ballad

William B. Rockwell & Norman Hedges

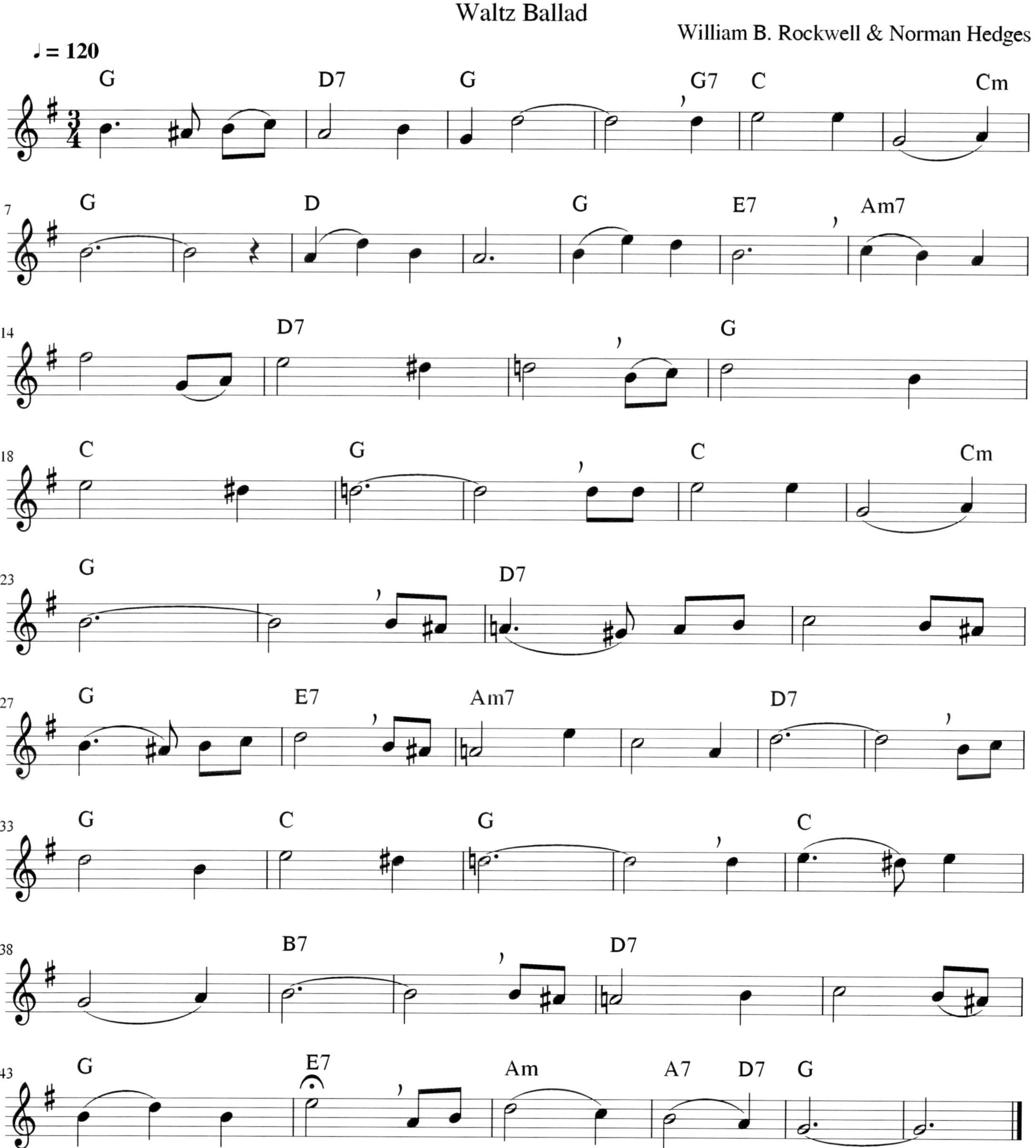

The Red River Valley

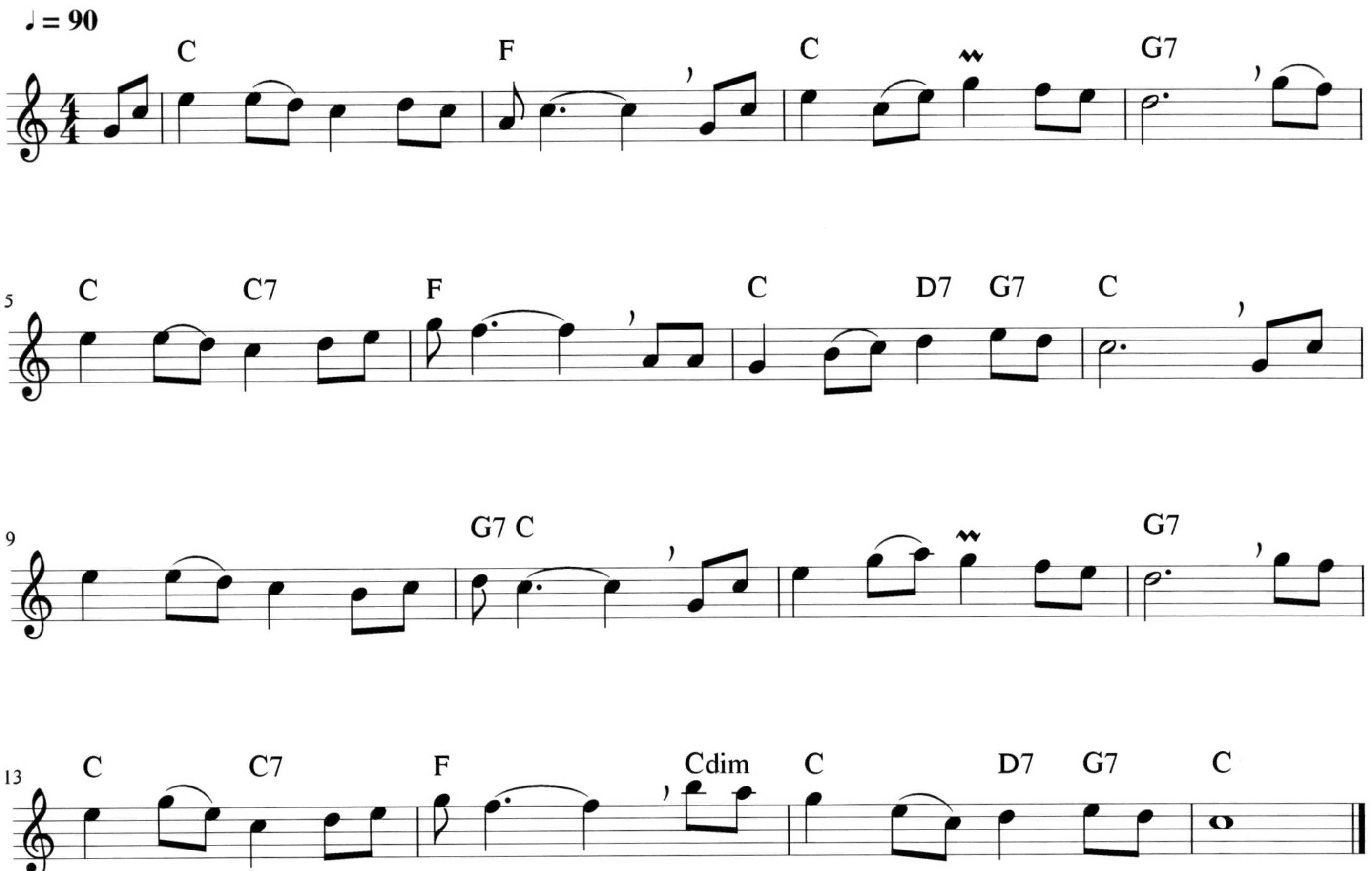

Am I Unforgiven Still?

1877

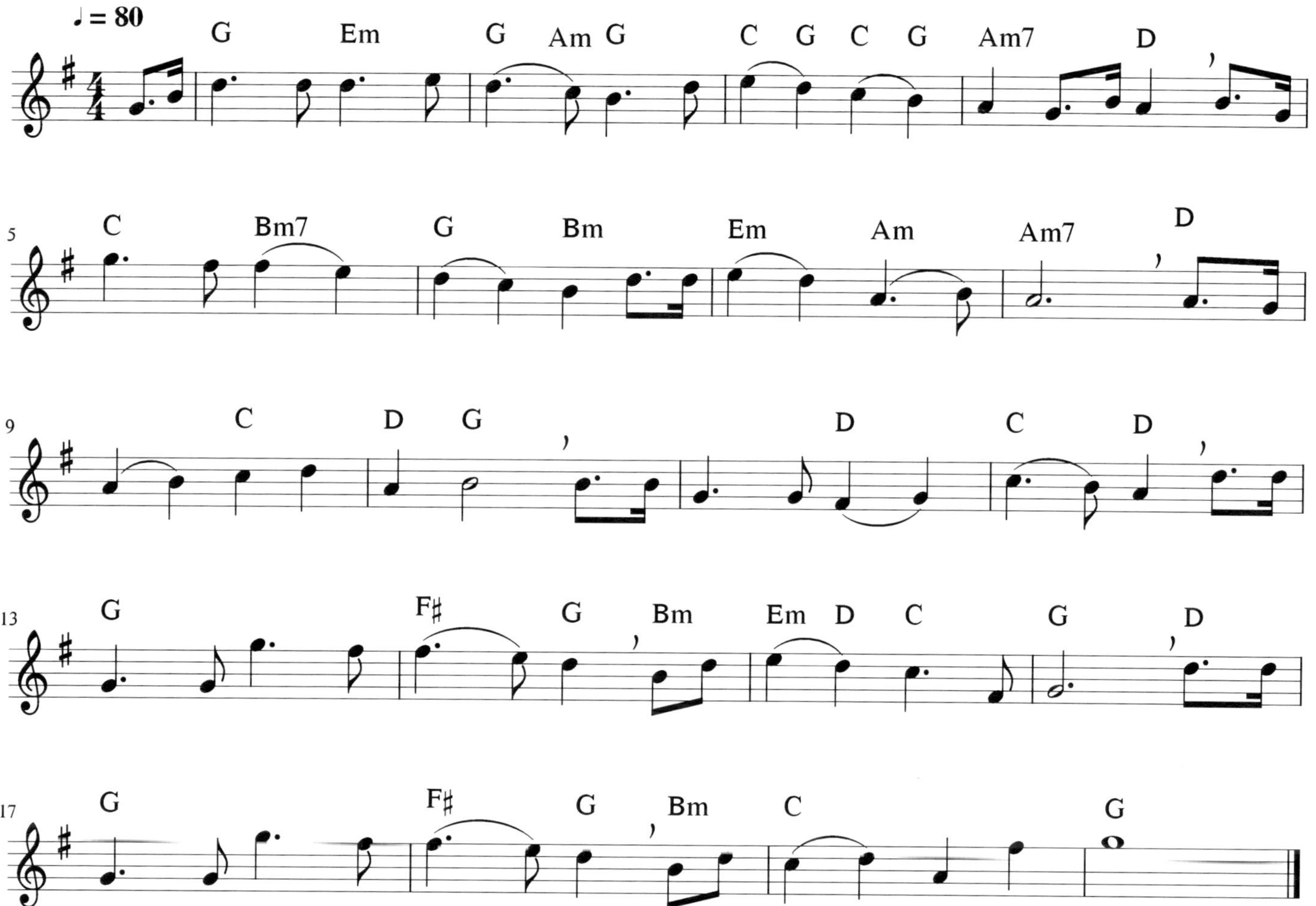

I'll Be All Smiles Tonight

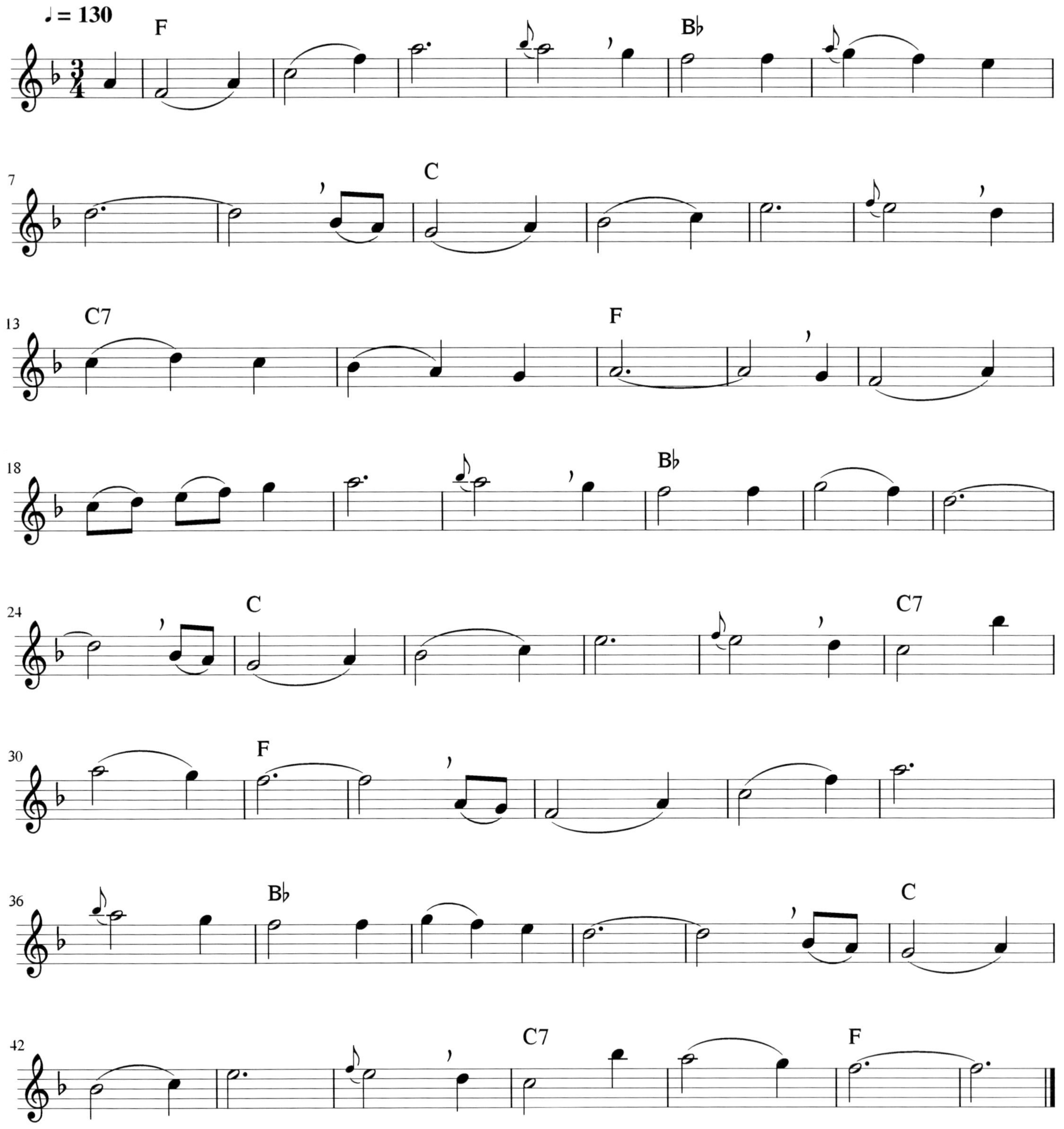

Black Is the Color of My True Love's Hair

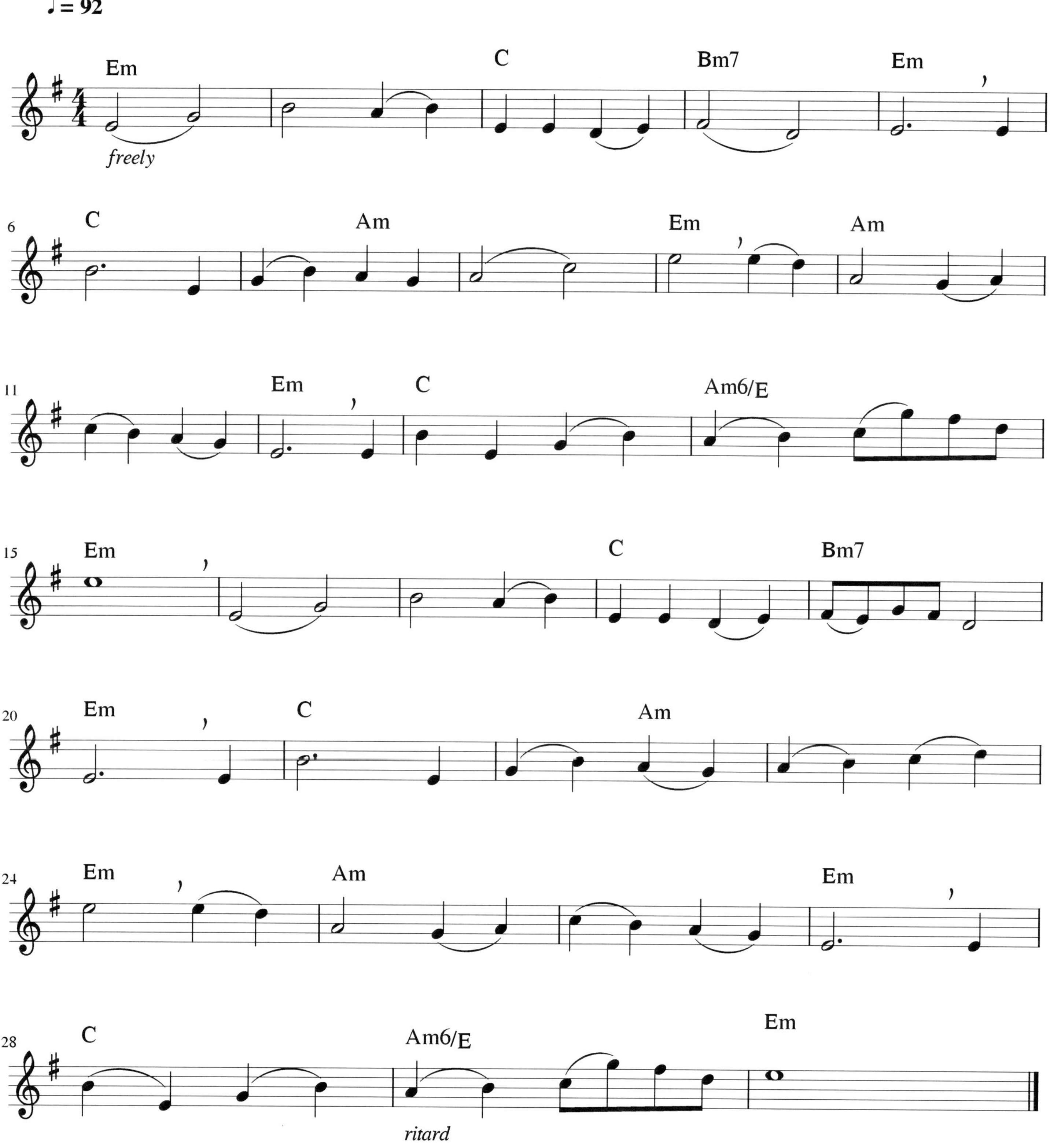

Just Awearyin' for You

Carrie Jacobs-Bond

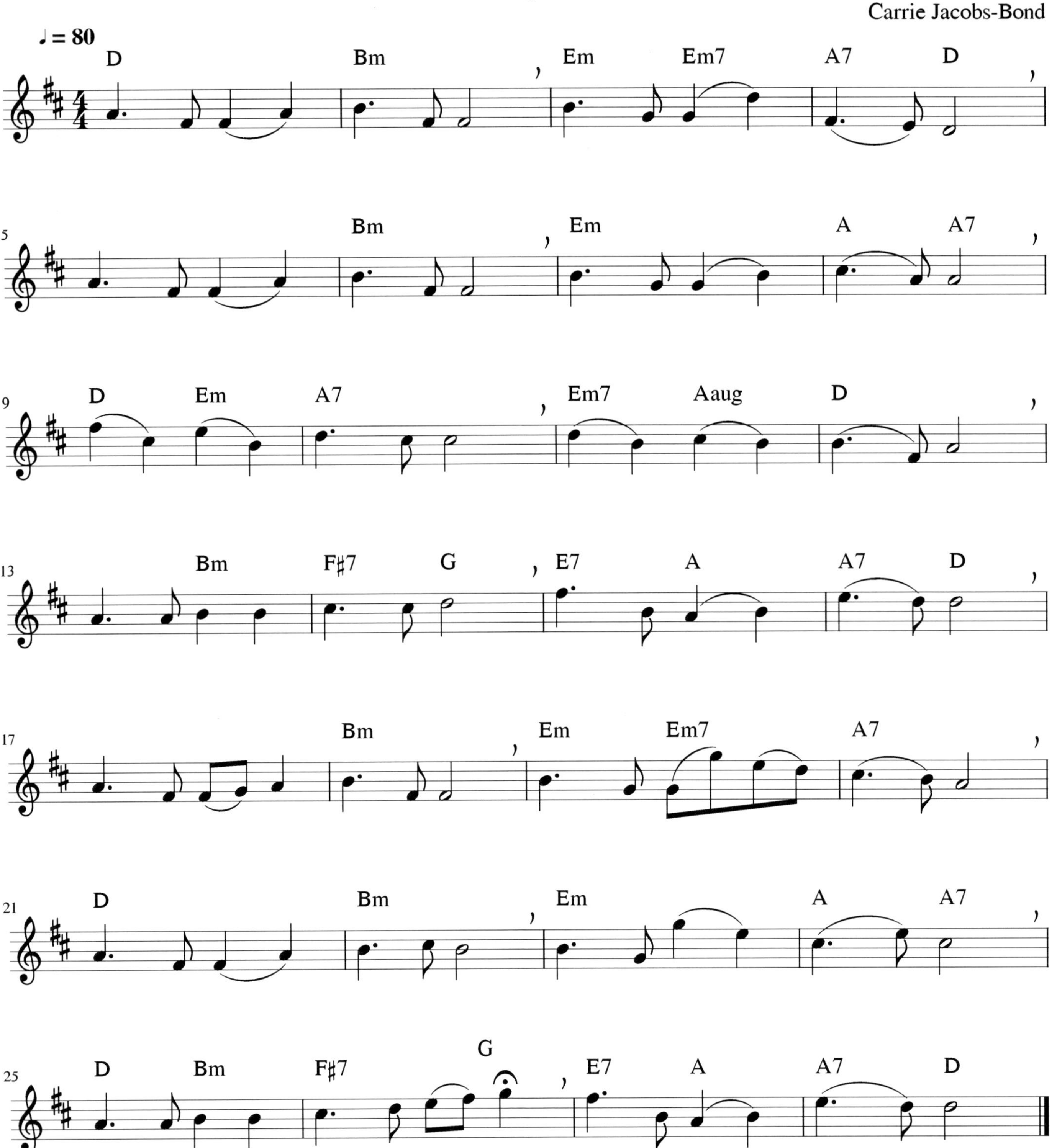

Aura Lee

♩ = 108
D E A7 D
5 E A7 D
9 D7 G Gm D
14 E7 A7 D E
19 A7 D E A7
24 D D7 G Gm D
29 E7 A7 D

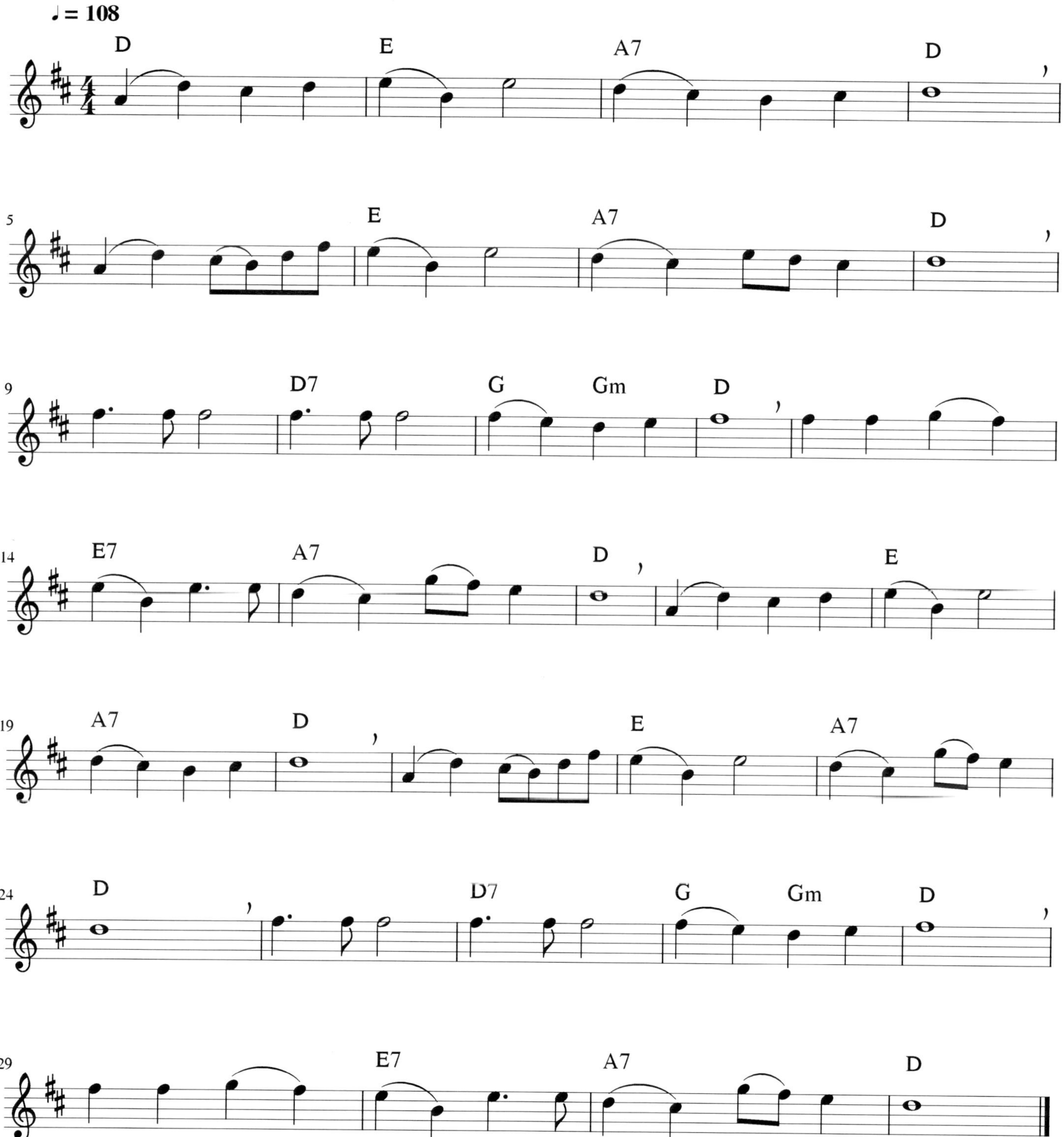

Farewell

Adieu

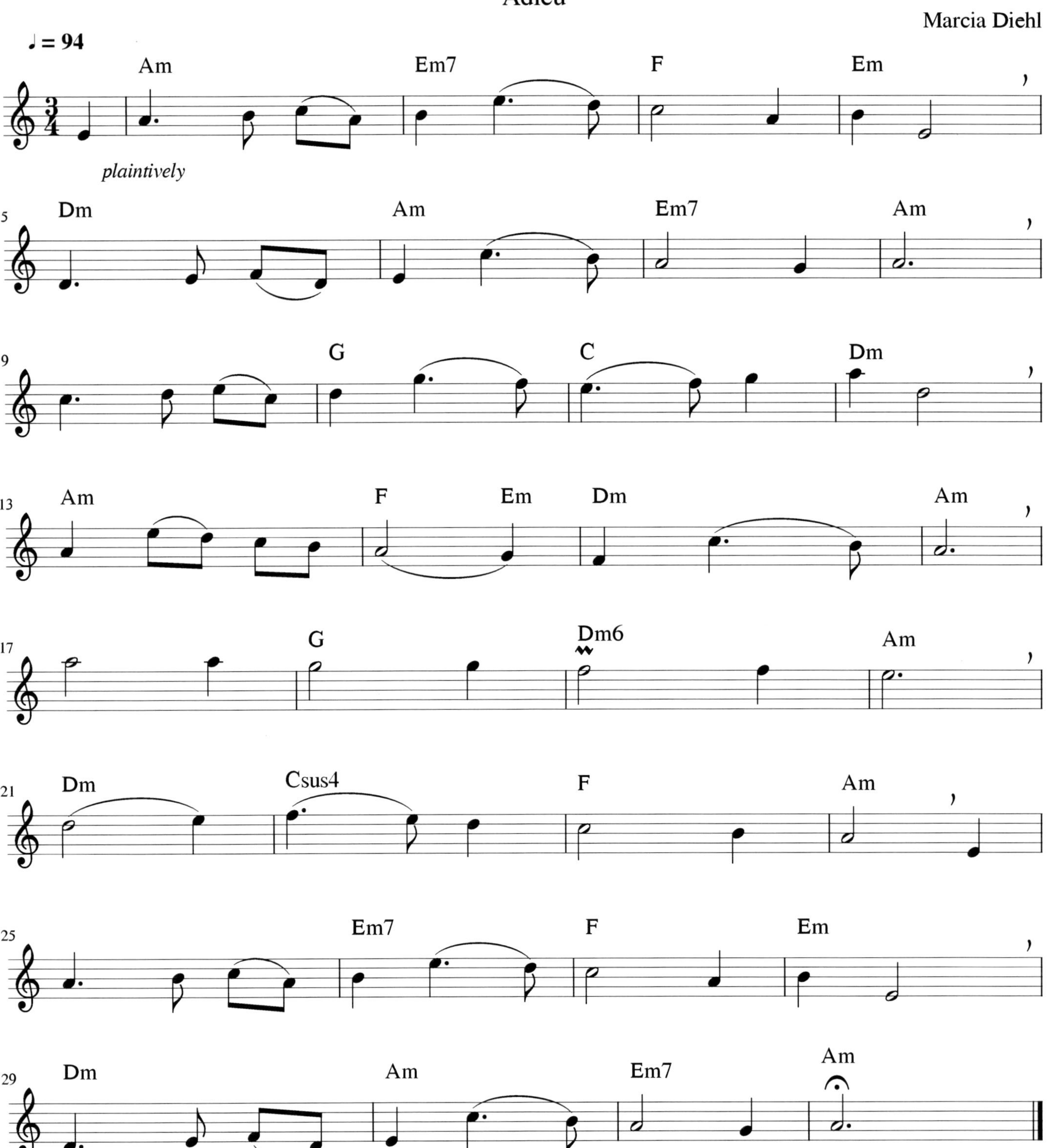